The Glorious Quran

Easy English Translation

Juz 30

Translated by
Mohammad Ali Khan

Copyrights © Mohammad Ali Khan 2024

All rights reserved.

All rights reserved. No part of this publication may be reproduced, distributed, or transmitted in any form or by any means, including photocopying, recording, or other electronic or mechanical methods, without the author's prior written permission, except in the case of brief quotations embodied in critical reviews and certain other non-commercial uses permitted by copyright law. For permission requests, please get in touch with the author.

Contents

Dedication..i
Acknowledgments... ii
About the Author.. iii
Preface.. iv
Sura An-Naba.. 1
Surat Al Naazia'at... 8
Sura A'basa... 16
Surat Al Takweer... 23
Sura Al Infitaar... 28
Sura al Muttaffifeen.. 31
Sura Inshiqaq.. 37
Sura Al Buruuj.. 41
Sura Al Tariq.. 45
Surat Al Aa'laa... 48
Surat Al Ghaashiah...51
Surat Al Fajr... 55
Surat Al Balad.. 60
Surat Al Shams... 64
Surat Al Lail... 67
Surat Al Duha... 71
Surat Al Inshirah... 73
Surat Al Theen... 75
Surat Al A'laq... 77
Surat Al Qadr..80
Surat Al Bayyina.. 81
Surat Al Zilzal.. 83
Surat Al A'adiyaat.. 85
Surat Al Qare'a...87
Surat At Takathur... 89
Surat Al A'sr... 91
Surat Al Humazah.. 92
Surat Al Feel.. 94
Surat Al Quraysh.. 95
Surat Al Maau'n... 96
Surat Al Kauthar.. 98
Surat Al Kafiroon... 99
Surat Al Nasr.. 101
Surat Al Masad... 102
Surat Al Ikhlaas.. 103
Surat Al Falaq...104
Surat Al Naas... 106

Dedication

Dedicated to all souls out there looking for the ultimate truth and ultimate guidance.

Acknowledgments

I learned this simple translation, word by word, as a child, from the late Syed Abdullah Shah of Mazara, Pakistan. May Allah bless his soul in Janat Ul Firdaus. I hereby acknowledge his greatest contribution to the learning of the holy Quran in its true original words and meanings, without any paraphrasing, to thousands of his pupils. Also, this simple translation was sent to many friends for feedback and corrections. I am thankful and acknowledge the efforts of Mr. Muzaffar Sheikh of Florida, Dr. Shafiq Ur Rahman of Florida, Mr. Nasir Awan of Delaware, and Dr. Farrukh Azmi of North Carolina for their guidance and feedback.

About the Author

Mohammad Ali Khan, a pediatrician by profession, loves to read the Holy Quran and enjoys the way it is recited and the way it sounds. He proclaims and pronounces Allah as the only creator and the only God worthy of worship. Allah takes human beings out from worshiping personalities, idols, wealth, national interest, tribal interest, self-interest, arrogance, self-worship, and self-praise and takes them into total obedience to Allah.

Preface

The Holy Quran has many translations in almost every language of the world. Sometimes, the meaning is confused, or the beauty of the scripture is lost in the translation. Sometimes, one word can not describe the meaning of the original word in the text.

The words of the Holy Quran are forever, not changeable, unique, and nothing is like these words anywhere in the world and no one can bring anything forward like this ever. The author thinks that translation should correspond to these words of the original text.

The meaning given to words of the Holy Quran can only be explained by the prophet Muhammad (peace be upon him). Any other explanation that is not reported or connected to the prophet (peace be upon him) or his companions (may Allah be pleased with all of them) may be the personal opinion of that person.

This simple translation is different in a few ways.

1. Meanings should correspond to the original words as closely as possible.
2. All pronouns should be explained as to whom those pronouns are referring to.
3. If one meaning is not doing justice to the original word, alternatives should be mentioned
4. Meanings should be simple and easy to understand for common people
5. Paraphrasing the meaning of the Quran should be avoided with an injection of thoughts and words not supported by the original text of the Glorious Quran.

6. Personal thoughts should be kept away; the words of Allah are enough for guidance.

7. Names of prophets should be mentioned as mentioned in the Quran with the same name and spelling mentioned in the Glorious Quran, not as mentioned elsewhere

8. Reference from other books and history must be avoided especially narrative mentioned in Christian and Jewish literature. The authenticity of those narratives and stories can not be confirmed.

9. The only reference acceptable is from Prophet Muhammad (peace be upon him) or his companions in the form of Sahih Hadith.

10. References from the scholars of later centuries, other than the explanation given by prophet Muhammad (peace be upon him) and his companions, are just their personal opinions, they may or may not be correct..

11. Scientific narrative must be kept away as those scientific facts may change with time, and the glorious Quran is not for the purpose of explaining science.

12. This book, the glorious Quran, is for all people, all generations till the day of judgment; new information available to current and future generations may help explain the word of the Quran better, as mentioned by prophet Muhammad (peace be upon him).

13. Personal explanations and opinions given by earlier scholars are not part of the original text, and this difference must be kept in mind.

14. Any extra explanation to make the meaning clear and easy is given in parenthesis and is not part of the original text. This difference must be kept in mind.

To connect with the author, Mohammad Ali Khan, please email shahab35@hotmail.com, phone 443-350-2359, Whatsapp 014433502359, X (formerly known as Twitter) account @khanmohammadali, hashtag #easyQuran.

Any guidance, comment or criticism from any person around the world regarding words and the accuracy of its meaning is highly appreciated. Any comment or suggestion will be replied to as much as possible.

سورة النبأ

Sura An-Naba

The Glorious Quran 78

بِسْمِ اللَّهِ الرَّحْمَٰنِ الرَّحِيمِ

(I begin) with the name of Allah, the Most Beneficent (Most Kind), the Most Merciful.

Aya 78-1
عَمَّ يَتَسَاءَلُونَ

From (about) what are they (disbelievers) asking? (One another).

Aya 78-2
عَنِ النَّبَإِ الْعَظِيمِ

From (about) the news, the great (big news)
(Big news of the message of Islam or the day of Resurrection).

Aya 78-3
الَّذِي هُمْ فِيهِ مُخْتَلِفُونَ

(The big news) the one (that) they (disbelievers) are in (about) it (the big news) disagreed (s) (disputing).

Aya 78-4
كَلَّا سَيَعْلَمُونَ

Nay (no, no, but) they (disbelievers) will soon (come to) know (the truth).

Aya 78-5
ثُمَّ كَلَّا سَيَعْلَمُونَ

Then, Nay (no, no, but), they (disbelievers) will soon (come to) know.

Aya 78-6
أَلَمْ نَجْعَلِ الْأَرْضَ مِهَادًا

Have not We (Allah) made the earth (as) cradle (resting place like a bed)?

Aya 78-7
وَالْجِبَالَ أَوْتَادًا

And (Allah made) the mountains (as its) pegs? (Stakes, bulwarks, to hold and stabilize the earth).

78-8
وَخَلَقْنَاكُمْ أَزْوَاجًا

And We (Allah) created you (all in) pairs (or different types).
(Male and female, or many different types of people).

78-9
وَجَعَلْنَا نَوْمَكُمْ سُبَاتًا

And We (Allah) made sleep of yours (as) resting.
(Respite or to take a break).

Aya 78-10
وَجَعَلْنَا اللَّيْلَ لِبَاسًا

And We (Allah) made the night (as) covering.
(Like a dress covering).

Aya 78-11
وَجَعَلْنَا النَّهَارَ مَعَاشًا

And We (Allah) made the day (for) livelihood.
(Business and living).

Aya 78-12
وَبَنَيْنَا فَوْقَكُمْ سَبْعًا شِدَادًا

And We (Allah) constructed (made) above you, seven strong (skies).

Aya 78-13
وَجَعَلْنَا سِرَاجًا وَهَّاجًا

And We (Allah) made lamp (sun) burning (shining, hot and blazing).

78-14
وَأَنزَلْنَا مِنَ الْمُعْصِرَاتِ مَاءً ثَجَّاجًا

And We (Allah) sent down from rain clouds (clouds laden with water or clouds with water dripping from it) water pouring (abundantly).

Aya 78-15
لِّنُخْرِجَ بِهِ حَبًّا وَنَبَاتًا

So that We (Allah) bring out with it (water) grain and plants (vegetation).

Aya 78-16
وَجَنَّاتٍ أَلْفَافًا

And gardens wrap around (entwined, dense, thick foliage layer upon layer).

Aya 78-17
إِنَّ يَوْمَ الْفَصْلِ كَانَ مِيقَاتًا

Surely, the Day of the Decision (Day of Judgment, or the day to separate true from false) was the appointment (appointed time).

Aya 78-18
يَوْمَ يُنفَخُ فِي الصُّورِ فَتَأْتُونَ أَفْوَاجًا

The day (of decision) will be blown into the trumpet, so you (all) will come (resurrected) in crowds (in groups).

Aya 78-19
وَفُتِحَتِ السَّمَاءُ فَكَانَتْ أَبْوَابًا

And opened (will be) the sky (heaven), so it will become doors (openings or gates).

Aya 78-20
وَسُيِّرَتِ الْجِبَالُ فَكَانَتْ سَرَابًا

And (that day of resurrection), moved will be (moving around) the mountains so they will become (a) mirage (optical illusion).

Aya 78:21
إِنَّ جَهَنَّمَ كَانَتْ مِرْصَادًا

Surely, Hell was in waiting (as a place of ambush, waiting for transgressors).

Aya 78:22
لِّلطَّاغِينَ مَآبًا

(Hell is) for transgressors (who cross the limits of Allah), the place of return (residence, abode).

Aya 78:23
لَّابِثِينَ فِيهَا أَحْقَابًا

Remaining (staying) in it (in the Hellfire for) ages (for a long time).

Aya 78:24
لَّا يَذُوقُونَ فِيهَا بَرْدًا وَلَا شَرَابًا

Not will they be tasting in it (in Hellfire) coolness and not (any) drink.

Aya 78:25
إِلَّا حَمِيمًا وَغَسَّاقًا

Except (for) boiling water and pus (purulence).

Aya 78:26
جَزَاءً وِفَاقًا

Reward (punishment) befitting (appropriate and proportionate to their evil deeds).

Aya 78:27
إِنَّهُمْ كَانُوا لَا يَرْجُونَ حِسَابًا

Surely, they were not expecting (an) account (to be held accountable on the Day of Judgment)

Aya 78:28
وَكَذَّبُوا بِآيَاتِنَا كِذَّابًا

And (they) belied (rejected) on signs of Ours (verses of Quran) (with) belying (rejecting or denying).

Aya 78:29
وَكُلَّ شَيْءٍ أَحْصَيْنَاهُ كِتَابًا

And everything We (Allah) counted (recorded) it (in) writing (in the book).

Aya 78:30
فَذُوقُوا فَلَن نَّزِيدَكُمْ إِلَّا عَذَابًا

So, (you all) taste (the punishment), so not, will We (Allah) increase for you except (in) punishment.

Aya 78:31
إِنَّ لِلْمُتَّقِينَ مَفَازًا

Surely, for the pious (righteous people who fear Allah and avoid sins for the fear of Allah) is the success.

Aya 78:32
حَدَائِقَ وَأَعْنَابًا

Gardens and grapes (grapevines).

Aya 78:33
وَكَوَاعِبَ أَتْرَابًا

And breasted companions of equal age (or splendid companions well matched).

Aya 78:34

وَكَأْسًا دِهَاقًا

And bowl full (overflowing with abundance).

Aya 78:35

لَّا يَسْمَعُونَ فِيهَا لَغْوًا وَلَا كِذَّابًا

Not will they (residents of paradise) hear in it (in paradise) useless talk and not (will they hear) lies (will not hear useless talk or falsehood).

Aya 78:36

جَزَاءً مِّن رَّبِّكَ عَطَاءً حِسَابًا

As (a) reward from the Lord of yours (Allah) as giving (gift based) on account (accounted for their good deeds).

Aya 78:37

رَّبِّ السَّمَاوَاتِ وَالْأَرْضِ وَمَا بَيْنَهُمَا الرَّحْمَٰنِ لَا يَمْلِكُونَ مِنْهُ خِطَابًا

The Lord (sustainer) of the skies (heaven) and the earth and whatever is in between these two, the Rahman (Allah-the Most Beneficent to all), not they own (have the power) from Him (from Allah), to address (to talk).

Aya 78:38

يَوْمَ يَقُومُ الرُّوحُ وَالْمَلَائِكَةُ صَفًّا لَّا يَتَكَلَّمُونَ إِلَّا مَنْ أَذِنَ لَهُ الرَّحْمَٰنُ وَقَالَ صَوَابًا

That day (of resurrection) will stand the spirit (angel Jibrael) and the angels in line (in row), not will they (angels) speak (talk) except the one permitted for him, (by) Rahman (the Most Beneficent Allah) and said the correct (truthful).

Aya 78:39

ذَٰلِكَ الْيَوْمُ الْحَقُّ فَمَن شَاءَ اتَّخَذَ إِلَىٰ رَبِّهِ مَآبًا

That (resurrection) day (is) the truth (confirmed and definite to come), so the one (who) wanted, he took toward Lord of his (Allah) return (return to obey and pray to Allah).

Aya 78:40

إِنَّا أَنذَرْنَاكُمْ عَذَابًا قَرِيبًا يَوْمَ يَنظُرُ الْمَرْءُ مَا قَدَّمَتْ يَدَاهُ وَيَقُولُ الْكَافِرُ يَا لَيْتَنِي كُنتُ تُرَابًا

Surely, We (Allah) warned you (all regarding a) punishment (that is) near, (that) day (of resurrection) will look at (see), the man to what sent forward (for hereafter) by two hands of his and will say the disbeliever "O, I wish, I was dust" (I wish that I was clay or earth than to face punishment).

سُوْرَةُ النَّزِعَٰتِ

Surat Al Naazia'at

The Glorious Quran 79

بِسْمِ اللَّهِ الرَّحْمَٰنِ الرَّحِيمِ

(I begin) with the name of Allah, the Most Beneficent (Most Kind), the Most Merciful.

Aya 79:1
وَالنَّازِعَاتِ غَرْقًا

And (swear) by extractors (pluckers, angels who extract souls at the time of death) drowning (with force and violence).
(Swear by angels who violently pull out the souls of the wicked and sinners).

Aya 79:2
وَالنَّاشِطَاتِ نَشْطًا

And (swear) by gentle angels, gentleness (ease).
(Swear by easy-going angels that draw out the souls easily and nicely of the believing people with good deeds at the time of death).

Aya 79:3
وَالسَّابِحَاتِ سَبْحًا

And (swear) by swimmers (angels or planets or objects that glide) swimming.
(Those angels or objects that glide like swimming and floating in space).

Aya 79:4
فَالسَّابِقَاتِ سَبْقًا

So overtakers (in doing good, like going ahead or pressing forward in a race to overtake) overtaking.

Aya 79:5
فَالْمُدَبِّرَاتِ أَمْرًا

So (those angels) planners (those angels that plan and arrange) the matter (affair, command, order).

Aya 79:6
يَوْمَ تَرْجُفُ الرَّاجِفَةُ

The day (the day of resurrection) will shake the shaking one (a violent earthquake will shake the earth at the first blowing of the trumpet).

Aya 79:7
تَتْبَعُهَا الرَّادِفَةُ

Will follow it (will follow the first shaker earthquake), the subsequent one (that comes afterward, another earthquake or the second blowing of the trumpet).

Aya 79:8
قُلُوبٌ يَوْمَئِذٍ وَاجِفَةٌ

Hearts on that day (of resurrection) will palpitate (shake with fear).

Aya 79:9
أَبْصَارُهَا خَاشِعَةٌ

Their eyes of it (of people) are cast down (humbled and full of fear).

Aya 79:10
يَقُولُونَ أَإِنَّا لَمَرْدُودُونَ فِي الْحَافِرَةِ

They (disbelievers) say, surely, we, definitely, are returners in the former state?
(Are we going to be resurrected back to life, like before?)

Aya 79:11
أَإِذَا كُنَّا عِظَامًا نَخِرَةً

Are (we will be resurrected) when we were bones decayed?
(Will we be resurrected when our bones crumble in pieces)?

Aya 79:12

قَالُوا تِلْكَ إِذًا كَرَّةٌ خَاسِرَةٌ

They (disbelievers) said this, then (at that time) will be a turn (recurrence, happening) loser (with loss or in vain or not likely, doubting the resurrection).

Aya 79:13

فَإِنَّمَا هِيَ زَجْرَةٌ وَاحِدَةٌ

So surely, it is shout (cry, blast) one (single or once, the sound of the second trumpet).

Aya 79:14

فَإِذَا هُم بِالسَّاهِرَةِ

So then, they will be on the awakening (awake or wakeful).

Aya 79:15

هَلْ أَتَاكَ حَدِيثُ مُوسَىٰ

Has come to you the talk (story or information) of (prophet) Musa (peace be upon him)?

Aya 79:16

إِذْ نَادَاهُ رَبُّهُ بِالْوَادِ الْمُقَدَّسِ طُوًى

When called upon him (Prophet Musa, peace be upon him), Lord of his (Allah) at the valley, the sacred (valley of) Tuwa.

Aya 79:17

اذْهَبْ إِلَىٰ فِرْعَوْنَ إِنَّهُ طَغَىٰ

Go toward Fir'aun, surely, he (Fir'aun) transgressed (disobeyed and crossed limits).

Aya 79:18

فَقُلْ هَل لَّكَ إِلَىٰ أَن تَزَكَّىٰ

So, say (O prophet Musa, peace be upon him, to Fir'aun), is there for you, (a way) toward that, you purify? (Will you purify and correct yourself?)

Aya 79:19
وَأَهْدِيَكَ إِلَىٰ رَبِّكَ فَتَخْشَىٰ

And I (prophet Musa, peace be upon him) guide you toward Lord of yours (Allah), so you fear (Allah).

Aya 79:20
فَأَرَاهُ الْآيَةَ الْكُبْرَىٰ

So, he (prophet Musa, peace be upon him) showed him (the Fir'aun) the sign (of Allah), the big (sign and great miracle from Allah).

Aya 79:21
فَكَذَّبَ وَعَصَىٰ

So, he (Fir'aun) belied (rejected the message and signs of Allah) and disobeyed (Allah).

Aya 79:22
ثُمَّ أَدْبَرَ يَسْعَىٰ

Then, he (Fir'aun) turned his back (refused to listen), running (in haste, trying his best to oppose).

Aya 79:23
فَحَشَرَ فَنَادَىٰ

So, he (Fir'aun) gathered (people) and so he shouted (pronounced and declared aloud in public).

Aya 79:24
فَقَالَ أَنَا رَبُّكُمُ الْأَعْلَىٰ

So, he (Fir'aun) said, I (Fir'aun) am, Lord of yours, the most high.

Aya 79:25
فَأَخَذَهُ اللَّهُ نَكَالَ الْآخِرَةِ وَالْأُولَىٰ

So, took (seized, punished) him, Allah, (making him an) example (deterrent lesson) for the later (life of hereafter) and the earlier (former worldly life).

Aya 79:26
إِنَّ فِي ذَٰلِكَ لَعِبْرَةً لِّمَن يَخْشَىٰ

Surely, in that (story), definitely is a lesson (to learn) for the one who fears (Allah).

Aya 79:27
أَأَنتُمْ أَشَدُّ خَلْقًا أَمِ السَّمَاءُ بَنَاهَا

Are you more intense (harder and more difficult) in creation or the sky? He (Allah) built it (made or constructed it).

Aya 79:28
رَفَعَ سَمْكَهَا فَسَوَّاهَا

He (Allah) raised the ceiling (vault, canopy, height) of it (of the sky), so He (Allah) equaled it (perfected and proportioned the sky).

Aya 79:29
وَأَغْطَشَ لَيْلَهَا وَأَخْرَجَ ضُحَاهَا

And He (Allah) darkened (made dark) night of it (of the sky) and brought out brightness (or forenoon) of it (of the sky).
(Made bright forenoon or the day).

Aya 79:30
وَالْأَرْضَ بَعْدَ ذَٰلِكَ دَحَاهَا

And the earth, after that, He (Allah) spread it (the earth).

Aya 79:31
أَخْرَجَ مِنْهَا مَاءَهَا وَمَرْعَاهَا

He (Allah) brought out from it (from the earth) water of it and grazing places of it (of the earth).
(Grazing places, pasture, land covered with grass).

Aya 79:32
وَالْجِبَالَ أَرْسَاهَا

And the mountains, He (Allah) firmly fixed it (as heavy firm weights on earth).

Aya 79:33

مَتَاعًا لَّكُمْ وَلِأَنْعَامِكُمْ

Benefit (provision) for you and for cattle (animals) of yours.

Aya 79:34

فَإِذَا جَاءَتِ الطَّامَّةُ الْكُبْرَىٰ

So, when came the calamity (catastrophe), the big one (the great calamity of the Day of Resurrection).

Aya 79:35

يَوْمَ يَتَذَكَّرُ الْإِنسَانُ مَا سَعَىٰ

(That) day (of resurrection) will remember the human, what he tried for (what he struggled for, and what his actions were).

Aya 79:36

وَبُرِّزَتِ الْجَحِيمُ لِمَن يَرَىٰ

And made upfront (made manifest, visible, and apparent in full view) the hellfire for the one who sees.

Aya 79:37

فَأَمَّا مَن طَغَىٰ

So, the one who transgressed (disobeyed Allah and crossed limits).

Aya 79:38

وَآثَرَ الْحَيَاةَ الدُّنْيَا

And preferred the life of the world. (Over the hereafter).

Aya 79:39

فَإِنَّ الْجَحِيمَ هِيَ الْمَأْوَىٰ

So surely, the hellfire is the place of living (abode or his home).

Aya 79:40

وَأَمَّا مَنْ خَافَ مَقَامَ رَبِّهِ وَنَهَى النَّفْسَ عَنِ الْهَوَىٰ

And the one who feared the place (status, power of Allah or fear standing in front of Allah) of the Lord of his (Allah) and forbade (prohibited, stopped) the nafs (self, himself) from the desire (lust).

Aya 79:41

فَإِنَّ الْجَنَّةَ هِيَ الْمَأْوَىٰ

So surely, the garden (paradise) is the place of living (home or abode for him).

Aya 79:42

يَسْأَلُونَكَ عَنِ السَّاعَةِ أَيَّانَ مُرْسَاهَا

They (disbelievers) ask you (O, prophet Muhammad, peace be upon him) from (about) the hour (day of resurrection), when is the arrival (occurrence) of it? (When will the day of resurrection come?)

Aya 79:43

فِيمَ أَنتَ مِن ذِكْرَاهَا

In what are you (O, Prophet Muhammad peace be upon him) from remembrance of it? (Knowledge or mention of the day of resurrection, meaning what you have to do with its mentioning?)

Aya 79:44

إِلَىٰ رَبِّكَ مُنتَهَاهَا

Toward the Lord of yours (Allah) is the end (final or ultimate knowledge) of it. (Allah has the ultimate knowledge of the day of resurrection).

Aya 79:45

إِنَّمَا أَنتَ مُنذِرُ مَن يَخْشَاهَا

Surely, you (O, Prophet Muhammad, peace be upon him) are (a) warner of the one who fears it (you can warn those who are afraid of the day of resurrection).

Aya 79:46

كَأَنَّهُمْ يَوْمَ يَرَوْنَهَا لَمْ يَلْبَثُوا إِلَّا عَشِيَّةً أَوْ ضُحَاهَا

Like, surely, they, (that) day, will see it (the day of resurrection) (will think) they did not stay (in the world or earlier life in graves) except an evening or forenoon of it.

سُوْرَةُ عَبَسَ

Sura A'basa

The Glorious Quran 80

بِسْمِ اللَّهِ الرَّحْمَٰنِ الرَّحِيمِ

(I begin) with the name of Allah, the Most Beneficent (Most Kind), the Most Merciful.

Aya 80:1
عَبَسَ وَتَوَلَّىٰ

Frowned and turned away (referring to Prophet Muhammad, peace be upon him).

Aya 80:2
أَن جَاءَهُ الْأَعْمَىٰ

That (because) came to him (to Prophet Muhammad peace be upon him) the blind (man, Abdullah bin Umm-Maktum, may Allah be pleased with him, the blind companion of the Prophet Peace be upon him, came and spoke, while the prophet peace be upon him was preaching to chiefs of Quraish).

Aya 80:3
وَمَا يُدْرِيكَ لَعَلَّهُ يَزَّكَّىٰ

And what makes you (O prophet, peace be upon him) know, perhaps he (the blind man) may purify (himself)?

Aya 80:4
أَوْ يَذَّكَّرُ فَتَنفَعَهُ الذِّكْرَىٰ

Or he (the blind man may) take the reminder (advice to the straight path), so will benefit him (the blind man) the reminder?

Aya 80.5
أَمَّا مَنِ اسْتَغْنَىٰ

As for the one (who) acted self-sufficiently (carefree or showed that he is aloof and does not care about guidance).

Aya 80.6
فَأَنتَ لَهُ تَصَدَّىٰ

So, you (O prophet Muhammad, peace be upon him), for him (for the one who does not care), you attended (addressed and paid attention).

Aya 80:7
وَمَا عَلَيْكَ أَلَّا يَزَّكَّىٰ

And not is, on you (any blame) that he (the carefree arrogant person) will not purify (himself or accept the truth).
(You are not responsible if they will not accept the message).

Aya 80:8
وَأَمَّا مَن جَاءَكَ يَسْعَىٰ

And the one (the blind companion, may Allah be pleased with him) who came to you running (striving and trying hard).

Aya 80:9
وَهُوَ يَخْشَىٰ

And he (the blind companion, may Allah be pleased with him) fears (Allah).

Aya 80:10
فَأَنتَ عَنْهُ تَلَهَّىٰ

So, you (O prophet Muhammad, peace be upon him) from him (from the blind companion, may Allah be pleased with him) diverted (yourself or ignored or distracted).

Aya 80:11
كَلَّا إِنَّهَا تَذْكِرَةٌ

Nay (no, no, but) surely, it (this Quran) is a reminder (advice).

Aya 80:12
فَمَن شَاءَ ذَكَرَهُ

So, whoever wanted, took the advice of it (remembrance of Quran)

Aya 80:13
فِي صُحُفٍ مُّكَرَّمَةٍ

(The reminder and advice is) in sheets (scrolls, books) honored (respected, Al-Lauh Al-Mahfuz-the main saved written manuscript book with Allah).

Aya 80:14
مَّرْفُوعَةٍ مُّطَهَّرَةٍ

Exalted (high and raised in dignity), purified.

Aya 80:15
بِأَيْدِي سَفَرَةٍ

In the hands of scribes (writing angels).

Aya 80:16
كِرَامٍ بَرَرَةٍ

(The writing angels) Noble (honorable) and pious (virtuous, righteous, dutiful).

Aya 80:17
قُتِلَ الْإِنسَانُ مَا أَكْفَرَهُ

(Is) killed (destroyed or cursed or death be to) the human, what made him reject. (What pride or achievement made the human reject the truth and be ungrateful?!)

Aya 80:18

مِنْ أَيِّ شَيْءٍ خَلَقَهُ

From what thing did He (Allah) create him?

Aya 80:19

مِن نُّطْفَةٍ خَلَقَهُ فَقَدَّرَهُ

From semen-drop, He (Allah) created him (the human), so (then) determined (proportioned, measured) him (the human).

Aya 80:20

ثُمَّ السَّبِيلَ يَسَّرَهُ

Then, the way (path of the birth canal), He (Allah) eased him (made easy for him, the birth process).

Aya 80:21

ثُمَّ أَمَاتَهُ فَأَقْبَرَهُ

Then He (Allah) made him (the human) die, so put him in (a) grave (provided him a grave).

Aya 80:22

ثُمَّ إِذَا شَاءَ أَنشَرَهُ

Then, when He (Allah) wanted (willed), He (Allah) resurrected him (on the Day of Judgment).

Aya 80:23

كَلَّا لَمَّا يَقْضِ مَا أَمَرَهُ

Nay (no, no, but), definitely, did not he (human) fulfill (done or accomplished) what He (Allah) ordered him (commanded him).

Aya 80:24

فَلْيَنظُرِ الْإِنسَانُ إِلَىٰ طَعَامِهِ

So, to (should) look the human toward food of his.

Aya 80:25
أَنَّا صَبَبْنَا الْمَاءَ صَبًّا

That, We (Allah) poured the water pouring (in abundance).

Aya 80:26
ثُمَّ شَقَقْنَا الْأَرْضَ شَقًّا

Then, We (Allah) split (cleaved) the earth splitting.

Aya 80:27
فَأَنبَتْنَا فِيهَا حَبًّا

So, We (Allah) grew (raised) in it (in the earth), the grain.

Aya 80:28
وَعِنَبًا وَقَضْبًا

And grapes and greens (herbage, clover).

Aya 80:29
وَزَيْتُونًا وَنَخْلًا

And olive and palm-tree.

Aya 80:30
وَحَدَائِقَ غُلْبًا

And gardens with dense trees (dense foliage and greenery).

Aya 80:31
وَفَاكِهَةً وَأَبًّا

And fruits and grass (fodder).

Aya 80:32
مَتَاعًا لَّكُمْ وَلِأَنْعَامِكُمْ

Benefit (provision) for you (humans) and for cattle of yours.

Aya 80:33
فَإِذَا جَاءَتِ الصَّاخَّةُ

So, when came the scream (shout or cry, deafening, piercing loud noise on the day of resurrection).

Aya 80:34
يَوْمَ يَفِرُّ الْمَرْءُ مِنْ أَخِيهِ

(That) the day will run away (flee) the man from the brother of his.

Aya 80:35
وَأُمِّهِ وَأَبِيهِ

And (will run away from) mother of his and father of his.

Aya 80:36
وَصَاحِبَتِهِ وَبَنِيهِ

And (will run away from) female companion (wife) of his and children of his.

Aya 80:37
لِكُلِّ امْرِئٍ مِّنْهُمْ يَوْمَئِذٍ شَأْنٌ يُغْنِيهِ

For every man, from them, that day will be a state (condition or situation) that will make him carefree (the situation will occupy him so much so as not to care about anyone).

Aya 80:38
وُجُوهٌ يَوْمَئِذٍ مُّسْفِرَةٌ

(Some) faces on that day (day of resurrection) will be bright (beaming, fresh, glowing).

Aya 80:39
ضَاحِكَةٌ مُّسْتَبْشِرَةٌ

Laughing and taking congratulations (rejoicing at the good news).

Aya 80:40
وَوُجُوهٌ يَوْمَئِذٍ عَلَيْهَا غَبَرَةٌ

And (some) faces on that day (of resurrection) upon it (faces), will be dust (covered with dust).

Aya 80:41
تَرْهَقُهَا قَتَرَةٌ

Will overcast (cover) it (the faces of theirs) darkness (miseries and gloom).

Aya 80:42
أُولَٰئِكَ هُمُ الْكَفَرَةُ الْفَجَرَةُ

Those (people with darkened faces) they are the disbelievers (rejectors of the truth and Quran), the sinners (wicked ones doing bad deeds).

سُورَةُ التَّكْوِيرِ

Surat Al Takweer

The Glorious Quran 81

بِسْمِ اللَّهِ الرَّحْمَٰنِ الرَّحِيمِ

(I begin) with the name of Allah, the Most Beneficent (Most Kind), the Most Merciful

Aya 81:1
إِذَا الشَّمْسُ كُوِّرَتْ

(On the day of resurrection) When the sun is covered (rolled, wrapped up).

Aya 81:2
وَإِذَا النُّجُومُ انكَدَرَتْ

And when the stars fall (lose their luster, dimmed, scattered, darken).

Aya 81:3
وَإِذَا الْجِبَالُ سُيِّرَتْ

And when the mountains are moved (made to move).

Aya 81:4
وَإِذَا الْعِشَارُ عُطِّلَتْ

And when the full-term pregnant she-camels are left unattended (abandoned, left alone, an example of valuable things abandoned).

Aya 81:5
وَإِذَا الْوُحُوشُ حُشِرَتْ

And when the wild animals will be gathered (for rewards of injustices to each other to enforce complete justice).

Aya 81:6
وَإِذَا الْبِحَارُ سُجِّرَتْ

And when the seas are set aflame (or overflow its banks).

Aya 81:7
وَإِذَا النُّفُوسُ زُوِّجَتْ

(On the day of resurrection) And when nufus (persons or souls) are paired (souls and bodies are united or people are grouped together).

Aya 81:8
وَإِذَا الْمَوْءُودَةُ سُئِلَتْ

And when the female infant buried alive will be asked (in ignorance times, female newborns used to be buried alive for shame).

Aya 81:9
بِأَيِّ ذَنبٍ قُتِلَتْ

For what sin was she killed?
(What was your sin, as a female newborn, to be buried alive for?)

Aya 81:10
وَإِذَا الصُّحُفُ نُشِرَتْ

And when the scrolls (books) are laid open (record books of deeds are opened to take accounts).

Aya 81:11
وَإِذَا السَّمَاءُ كُشِطَتْ

(On the day of resurrection) And when the sky is stripped (torn away or the covering taken off).

Aya 81:12
وَإِذَا الْجَحِيمُ سُعِّرَتْ

And when the hellfire is set ablaze (kindled to full blaze).

Aya 81:13
وَإِذَا الْجَنَّةُ أُزْلِفَتْ

And when Paradise is brought near (brought into view).

Aya 81:14
عَلِمَتْ نَفْسٌ مَّا أَحْضَرَتْ

Will know every nafs (person or soul), what it has brought (to the hereafter, good or bad deeds).

Aya 81:15
فَلَا أُقْسِمُ بِالْخُنَّسِ

So, no, I (Allah) swear by the retreating (stars or planets that recede, rise, and fall).

Aya 81:16
الْجَوَارِ الْكُنَّسِ

(Planets or stars) the runners (moving swiftly) the disappearer (hide from vision).

Aya 81:17
وَاللَّيْلِ إِذَا عَسْعَسَ

And (swear) by the night when it departed (ended, darkened).

Aya 81:18
وَالصُّبْحِ إِذَا تَنَفَّسَ

And (swear by) the morning (Dawn) when it breathed (started).

Aya 81:19
إِنَّهُ لَقَوْلُ رَسُولٍ كَرِيمٍ

Surely, it is (Quran) definitely, the word of the noble messenger (angel Jibrael, who brought the revelation).

Aya 81:20

ذِي قُوَّةٍ عِندَ ذِي الْعَرْشِ مَكِينٍ

(Angel Jibrael) Owner of power, with the Owner of the Arsh (throne of Allah) having (a) place (having high status with Allah, established).

Aya 81:21

مُطَاعٍ ثَمَّ أَمِينٍ

Obeyed (angel Jibrael is obeyed by other angels) there (with Allah and is) trustworthy.

Aya 81:22

وَمَا صَاحِبُكُم بِمَجْنُونٍ

And not is, companion of yours (Prophet Muhammad, Peace be upon him) a madman.

Aya 81:23

وَلَقَدْ رَآهُ بِالْأُفُقِ الْمُبِينِ

And surely, he (Prophet Muhammad, peace be upon him) saw him (the angel Jibrael) on the horizon, the clear (horizon).

Aya 81:24

وَمَا هُوَ عَلَى الْغَيْبِ بِضَنِينٍ

And not is he (prophet Muhammad, peace be upon him) on the unseen (knowledge of the hidden things) withholder (by not telling you and withholding knowledge of the unseen).

Aya 81:25

وَمَا هُوَ بِقَوْلِ شَيْطَانٍ رَّجِيمٍ

And not is it (this Quran) the word of Shaitaan (devil), the accursed (rejected devil).

Aya 81:26

فَأَيْنَ تَذْهَبُونَ

So where are you going? (By not believing in the Quran.)

Aya 81:27
إِنْ هُوَ إِلَّا ذِكْرٌ لِّلْعَالَمِينَ

Not is it (this Quran) except a reminder (advice and guidance) for the universes (worlds, mankind, and jinn).

Aya 81:28
لِمَن شَاءَ مِنكُمْ أَن يَسْتَقِيمَ

For the one wanted from (amongst) you, that he to go straight (to get the straight path of guidance from the Quran).

Aya 81:29
وَمَا تَشَاءُونَ إِلَّا أَن يَشَاءَ اللَّهُ رَبُّ الْعَالَمِينَ

And not you (all) can want (intend) except that, what wants (intends, wills) Allah, the Lord of the universes (Worlds).

سُوْرَةُ الْاِنْفِطَارِ

Sura Al Infitaar

The Glorious Quran 82

بِسْمِ اللَّهِ الرَّحْمَٰنِ الرَّحِيمِ

(I begin) with the name of Allah, the Most Beneficent (Most Kind), the Most Merciful.

Aya 82:1
إِذَا السَّمَاءُ انفَطَرَتْ

(On the day of resurrection)
When the sky is broken into pieces (cleft asunder).

Aya 82:1
وَإِذَا الْكَوَاكِبُ انتَثَرَتْ

And when the stars are scattered (dispersed).

Aya 82:3
وَإِذَا الْبِحَارُ فُجِّرَتْ

And when the seas are made to burst (gush beyond their banks).

Aya 82:4
وَإِذَا الْقُبُورُ بُعْثِرَتْ

And when the graves are overturned (laid open or made upside down and people in graves are resurrected).

Aya 82:5
عَلِمَتْ نَفْسٌ مَّا قَدَّمَتْ وَأَخَّرَتْ

Will know nafs (every person, soul) what it has sent forth and (what) it left behind.

Aya 82:6
يَا أَيُّهَا الْإِنسَانُ مَا غَرَّكَ بِرَبِّكَ الْكَرِيمِ

O you, the human, what deceived you, on (concerning) Lord of yours (Allah), the Most Noble? (Generous, Bountiful).

Aya 82:7
الَّذِي خَلَقَكَ فَسَوَّاكَ فَعَدَلَكَ

The One (Allah, who) created you, so fashioned (completed or adjusted) you, then balanced (equaled, proportioned) you.

Aya 82:8
فِي أَيِّ صُورَةٍ مَّا شَاءَ رَكَّبَكَ

In whatever form that He (Allah) wanted (willed), He (Allah) assembled (constituted) you.

Aya 82:9
كَلَّا بَلْ تُكَذِّبُونَ بِالدِّينِ

Nay (no, no, but), but you are belying (rejecting or denying) on the Deen (religion of Allah or the judgment day).

Aya 82:10
وَإِنَّ عَلَيْكُمْ لَحَافِظِينَ

And surely, over you, definitely, are protectors (guardian angels).

Aya 82:11
كِرَامًا كَاتِبِينَ

Honorable (noble) writers (recorders of your deeds).

Aya 82:12
يَعْلَمُونَ مَا تَفْعَلُونَ

They (writing angels) know whatever you (all) do.

Aya 82:13
إِنَّ الْأَبْرَارَ لَفِي نَعِيمٍ

Surely, the righteous (people with good deeds) definitely, definitely will be in blessings (bounties of paradise).

Aya 82:14
وَإِنَّ الْفُجَّارَ لَفِي جَحِيمٍ

And surely, the evil doers (wicked sinners) definitely, will be in hellfire.

Aya 82:15
يَصْلَوْنَهَا يَوْمَ الدِّينِ

They will reach (enter) it (the hell on) the day of Deen (day of judgment)

Aya 82:16
وَمَا هُمْ عَنْهَا بِغَائِبِينَ

And not are they (evildoers) from it (from hellfire, to be) absent (they cannot run away from it).

Aya 82:17
وَمَا أَدْرَاكَ مَا يَوْمُ الدِّينِ

And what made you know what is the day of Deen (the day of judgment)?

Aya 82:18
ثُمَّ مَا أَدْرَاكَ مَا يَوْمُ الدِّينِ

Again, what made you know what is the day of Deen (the day of judgment)?

Aya 82:19
يَوْمَ لَا تَمْلِكُ نَفْسٌ لِنَفْسٍ شَيْئًا وَالْأَمْرُ يَوْمَئِذٍ لِلَّهِ

(The) Day (that day of judgment) will not own (will not have power) any nafs (any person) for (another) nafs (person) anything, and the order (power, command, and authority) that day will be only for Allah.

سورة المطفّفين

Sura al Muttaffifeen

The Glorious Quran 83

بِسْمِ اللَّهِ الرَّحْمَٰنِ الرَّحِيمِ

(I begin) with the name of Allah, the Most Beneficent (Most Kind), the Most Merciful.

Aya 83:1
وَيْلٌ لِّلْمُطَفِّفِينَ

Woe (destruction) is for the givers of less (defrauders, who give less while measuring weight or length in buying and selling).

Aya 83:2
الَّذِينَ إِذَا اكْتَالُوا عَلَى النَّاسِ يَسْتَوْفُونَ

Those (people) who, when they take measures on people (receive measures from people), they take full (measures)

Aya 83:3
وَإِذَا كَالُوهُمْ أَو وَّزَنُوهُمْ يُخْسِرُونَ

And when they measure (for) them (other people) or weigh (to give) for them (to other people), they give less (than expected correct weight or scale).

Aya 83:4
أَلَا يَظُنُّ أُولَٰئِكَ أَنَّهُم مَّبْعُوثُونَ

Do not they think (consider) those (people) that they will be resurrected.

Aya 83:5
لِيَوْمٍ عَظِيمٍ

For the day great (big day of judgment).

Aya 83:6
يَوْمَ يَقُومُ النَّاسُ لِرَبِّ الْعَالَمِينَ

(The) Day (of judgment) will stand the people, for the Lord of universes (in front of Allah, the Lord of all worlds).

Aya 83:7
كَلَّا إِنَّ كِتَابَ الْفُجَّارِ لَفِي سِجِّينٍ

Nay (no, no, but), surely, the book (record of deeds) of sinners (ill-doers and wicked people) is definitely in the Sijjin.

Aya 83:8
وَمَا أَدْرَاكَ مَا سِجِّينٌ

And what made you know what "Sijjin" is?

Aya 83:9
كِتَابٌ مَّرْقُومٌ

Book written.

Aya 83:10
وَيْلٌ يَوْمَئِذٍ لِّلْمُكَذِّبِينَ

Woe (destruction) is that day for the beliers (deniers, rejectors).

Aya 83:11
الَّذِينَ يُكَذِّبُونَ بِيَوْمِ الدِّينِ

Those (people) who belie (deny, reject) the day of judgment.

Aya 83:12
وَمَا يُكَذِّبُ بِهِ إِلَّا كُلُّ مُعْتَدٍ أَثِيمٍ

And not will belie (deny) on it (the day of judgment) except every transgressor, sinner (who crosses limits and is sinful).

Aya 83:13
إِذَا تُتْلَىٰ عَلَيْهِ آيَاتُنَا قَالَ أَسَاطِيرُ الْأَوَّلِينَ

When are recited on him, signs of ours (verses of Quran), he said, lines of the earlier (people) (stories of ancient people).

Aya 83:14
كَلَّا ۖ بَلْ ۜ رَانَ عَلَىٰ قُلُوبِهِم مَّا كَانُوا يَكْسِبُونَ

Nay (no, no, but) but stained (rusted) on hearts of theirs, what (due to) they were earning (bad deeds that they were doing).

Aya 83:15
كَلَّا إِنَّهُمْ عَن رَّبِّهِمْ يَوْمَئِذٍ لَّمَحْجُوبُونَ

Nay (no, no, but), surely, they from the Lord of theirs (Allah), that day (of judgment), definitely, will be veiled (debarred).

Aya 83:16
ثُمَّ إِنَّهُمْ لَصَالُو الْجَحِيمِ

Then, surely, they are reaching (entering) the Hellfire.

Aya 83:17
ثُمَّ يُقَالُ هَٰذَا الَّذِي كُنتُم بِهِ تُكَذِّبُونَ

Then, it will be said (to them, this is the one (hellfire) that you were on it (this hellfire) belying (denying).

Aya 83:18
كَلَّا إِنَّ كِتَابَ الْأَبْرَارِ لَفِي عِلِّيِّينَ

Nay (no, no, but), surely, the book (of record) of the righteous (people who believed and did good deeds), definitely, will be in the "Illyyun"

Aya 83:19
وَمَا أَدْرَاكَ مَا عِلِّيُّونَ

And what made you know what 'Illiyyun' is?

Aya 83:20

كِتَابٌ مَّرْقُومٌ

Book written.

Aya 83:21

يَشْهَدُهُ الْمُقَرَّبُونَ

Will witness it (the book of deed) the nearest (people nearest to Allah).

Aya 83:22

إِنَّ الْأَبْرَارَ لَفِي نَعِيمٍ

Surely, the righteous (the pious people), definitely, will be in blessings (provisions, bounties of paradise).

Aya 83:23

عَلَى الْأَرَائِكِ يَنظُرُونَ

On thrones (couches) watching (looking on and observing).

Aya 83:24

تَعْرِفُ فِي وُجُوهِهِمْ نَضْرَةَ النَّعِيمِ

You will know (see or recognize) in faces of theirs, the brightness (freshness or joy) of the blessings (bounties of paradise).

Aya 83:25

يُسْقَوْنَ مِن رَّحِيقٍ مَّخْتُومٍ

They (residents of paradise) will be given to drink from drink sealed (pure nectar drink).

Aya 83:26

خِتَامُهُ مِسْكٌ وَفِي ذَٰلِكَ فَلْيَتَنَافَسِ الْمُتَنَافِسُونَ

The seal of (that drink) will be the (smell of) musk, and in that (paradise and bounties of it), so should compete (struggle, strive) the competitors (strivers).

Aya 83:27

وَمِزَاجُهُ مِن تَسْنِيمٍ

And mixture of it (with that drink) will be (water) from (the spring of) Tasneem.

Aya 83:28

عَيْنًا يَشْرَبُ بِهَا الْمُقَرَّبُونَ

(Tasneem is) A fountain (spring) that drink from it, the nearest (people, close to Allah)

Aya 83:29

إِنَّ الَّذِينَ أَجْرَمُوا كَانُوا مِنَ الَّذِينَ آمَنُوا يَضْحَكُونَ

Surely, those (people who) committed crimes (in worldly life), they were, from those (people who) believed (in Allah and the Quran), laughing (in joking and mocking).

Aya 83:30

وَإِذَا مَرُّوا بِهِمْ يَتَغَامَزُونَ

And when they (criminal disbelievers) passed by them (by true believers) they were winking (at one another, in mockery of the believers).

Aya 83:31

وَإِذَا انقَلَبُوا إِلَىٰ أَهْلِهِمُ انقَلَبُوا فَكِهِينَ

And when they (criminal disbelievers) returned to families of theirs, they returned, jesting (enjoying their joking or ridiculing or taunting).

Aya 83:32

وَإِذَا رَأَوْهُمْ قَالُوا إِنَّ هَٰؤُلَاءِ لَضَالُّونَ

And when they (criminal disbelievers) saw them (the true believers), they said, surely, these (true believers) are definitely misguided (people gone astray or wrong).

Aya 83:33

وَمَا أُرْسِلُوا عَلَيْهِمْ حَافِظِينَ

And not were they (criminal disbelievers) sent on them (on true believers as) protectors (guardians, watchers).

Aya 83:34
فَالْيَوْمَ الَّذِينَ آمَنُوا مِنَ الْكُفَّارِ يَضْحَكُونَ

So today (on the day of judgment) those (who) believed (in Allah and Quran), from (on) the disbelievers, will be laughing (as a mocking)

Aya 83:35
عَلَى الْأَرَائِكِ يَنظُرُونَ

(Resting in paradise) On thrones (couches) looking (seeing or watching or gazing).

Aya 83:36
هَلْ ثُوِّبَ الْكُفَّارُ مَا كَانُوا يَفْعَلُونَ

Have been rewarded (paid back) the disbelievers (for) what they were doing (in the worldly life)?

سُورَةُ الْاِنْشِقَاقِ

Sura Inshiqaq

The Glorious Quran 84

بِسْمِ اللَّهِ الرَّحْمَٰنِ الرَّحِيمِ

(I begin) with the name of Allah, the Most Beneficent (Most Kind), the Most Merciful.

Aya 84:1
إِذَا السَّمَاءُ انشَقَّتْ

When the sky split apart (burst apart, rent asunder on the day of judgment).

Aya 84:2
وَأَذِنَتْ لِرَبِّهَا وَحُقَّتْ

And it (the sky) responded (listened to, obeyed) for the Lord of its (Lord of the sky, Allah), and was truly bound to (was rightly obligated to do so).

Aya 84:3
وَإِذَا الْأَرْضُ مُدَّتْ

And when the earth is stretched (spread or leveled on the day of judgment).

Aya 84:4
وَأَلْقَتْ مَا فِيهَا وَتَخَلَّتْ

And has thrown out (cast out) what is in it (inside the earth) and is emptied (on the day of judgment).

Aya 84:5
وَأَذِنَتْ لِرَبِّهَا وَحُقَّتْ

And it (the earth) responded (listened to, obeyed) for the Lord of its (Lord of the earth, Allah), and was truly bound to (was rightly obligated to do so).

Aya 84:6
يَا أَيُّهَا الْإِنسَانُ إِنَّكَ كَادِحٌ إِلَىٰ رَبِّكَ كَدْحًا فَمُلَاقِيهِ

O you, the human (mankind), surely, you (the human) are struggler hard (laboring with hardship) toward the Lord of yours (Allah) struggle (labor), so you will meet Him (Allah).

Aya 84:7
فَأَمَّا مَنْ أُوتِيَ كِتَابَهُ بِيَمِينِهِ

So, the one who is given book (of deeds) of his with the right hand of his.

Aya 84:8
فَسَوْفَ يُحَاسَبُ حِسَابًا يَسِيرًا

So soon, he will be accounted (his accounts will be completed) , accounting easy.

Aya 84:9
وَيَنقَلِبُ إِلَىٰ أَهْلِهِ مَسْرُورًا

And he will return to the family of his, happy.

Aya 84:10
وَأَمَّا مَنْ أُوتِيَ كِتَابَهُ وَرَاءَ ظَهْرِهِ

And the one who is given book (of deeds) of his, behind back of his.

Aya 84:11
فَسَوْفَ يَدْعُو ثُبُورًا

So soon, he will call (for his) destruction.

Aya 84:12
وَيَصْلَىٰ سَعِيرًا

And will reach (enter) the blaze (fire).

Aya 84:13

إِنَّهُ كَانَ فِي أَهْلِهِ مَسْرُورًا

Surely, he was in the family of his, happy (in the worldly life).

Aya 84:14

إِنَّهُ ظَنَّ أَن لَّن يَحُورَ

Surely, he thought (assumed) that never will he return (come back to Allah for accounts on the day of judgment).

Aya 84:15

بَلَىٰ إِنَّ رَبَّهُ كَانَ بِهِ بَصِيرًا

Yea, surely, Lord of his (Allah) was over him, Seer (watching).

Aya 84:16

فَلَا أُقْسِمُ بِالشَّفَقِ

So no, I (Allah) swear by the Afterglow (the twilight glow or light on the horizon after the sunset).

Aya 84:17

وَاللَّيْلِ وَمَا وَسَقَ

And (I swear) on the night and what it (the night) envelops (hide in itself).

Aya 84:18

وَالْقَمَرِ إِذَا اتَّسَقَ

And (I swear) by the moon when it (the moon) becomes full.

Aya 84:19

لَتَرْكَبُنَّ طَبَقًا عَن طَبَقٍ

Definitely, you will ascend (embark or enter) stage from (a) stage (life before birth to worldly life to life in the grave and then hereafter).

Aya 84:20
فَمَا لَهُمْ لَا يُؤْمِنُونَ

So what is (the matter) for them (disbelievers), not they believe (In Allah)?

Aya 84:21
وَإِذَا قُرِئَ عَلَيْهِمُ الْقُرْآنُ لَا يَسْجُدُونَ ۩

And when is recited on them, the Quran, not they prostrate (they do not do sajdah to Allah).
(Aya of Sajdah, must do sajdah).

Aya 84:22
بَلِ الَّذِينَ كَفَرُوا يُكَذِّبُونَ

But, those who disbelieved, they belie (deny, reject the truth).

Aya 84:23
وَاللَّهُ أَعْلَمُ بِمَا يُوعُونَ

And Allah is the most knowing, on what they hide (keep hidden in their hearts).

Aya 84:24
فَبَشِّرْهُم بِعَذَابٍ أَلِيمٍ

So, give them (disbelievers) the good news of punishment painful.

Aya 84:25
إِلَّا الَّذِينَ آمَنُوا وَعَمِلُوا الصَّالِحَاتِ لَهُمْ أَجْرٌ غَيْرُ مَمْنُونٍ

Except those who believed (in Islam) and did good deeds, for them is (a) reward never ending.

سُوۡرَةُ الۡبُرُوۡجِ

Sura Al Buruuj

The Glorious Quran 85

بِسۡمِ اللَّهِ الرَّحۡمٰنِ الرَّحِيۡمِ

(I begin) with the name of Allah, the Most Beneficent (Most Kind), the Most Merciful.

Aya 85:1
وَالسَّمَاءِ ذَاتِ الۡبُرُوۡجِ

By (I swear) the sky with (owner of) the constellations (or big mansions of stars).

Aya 85:2
وَالۡيَوۡمِ الۡمَوۡعُوۡدِ

And (I swear) by the day, the promised (day of resurrection).

Aya 85:3
وَشَاهِدٍ وَمَشۡهُوۡدٍ

And (I swear) by the witness and (what is) witnessed.

Aya 85:4
قُتِلَ أَصۡحَابُ الۡأُخۡدُوۡدِ

Got killed (destroyed, be cursed) the companions of the ditch (people who made that trench or pit for burning the true believers).

(Ditch in which true believers were burned alive).

Aya 85:5
النَّارِ ذَاتِ الۡوَقُوۡدِ

The fire with fuel.

Aya 85:6

إِذْ هُمْ عَلَيْهَا قُعُودٌ

When they (cruel disbelievers) were on it (on the side of the fire ditch), sitting.

Aya 85:7

وَهُمْ عَلَىٰ مَا يَفْعَلُونَ بِالْمُؤْمِنِينَ شُهُودٌ

And they (cruel disbelievers) were, over what they were doing to the (true) believers, witnesses.
(They were watching them burn.)

Aya 85:8

وَمَا نَقَمُوا مِنْهُمْ إِلَّا أَن يُؤْمِنُوا بِاللَّهِ الْعَزِيزِ الْحَمِيدِ

And not they took revenge from them (from those true believers) except (for) that they believed in Allah, the All-Mighty, the Praiseworthy.

Aya 85:9

الَّذِي لَهُ مُلْكُ السَّمَاوَاتِ وَالْأَرْضِ وَاللَّهُ عَلَىٰ كُلِّ شَيْءٍ شَهِيدٌ

The one (Allah) for Him is the kingdom of the skies (heavens) and the earth; and Allah is, on every (all) thing, witness.

Aya 85:10

إِنَّ الَّذِينَ فَتَنُوا الْمُؤْمِنِينَ وَالْمُؤْمِنَاتِ ثُمَّ لَمْ يَتُوبُوا فَلَهُمْ عَذَابُ جَهَنَّمَ وَلَهُمْ عَذَابُ الْحَرِيقِ

Surely, those who tried (put into trial or persecuted) the believer men and the believer women, then, not they repent (to Allah), so for them is the punishment of hell, and for them is the punishment of fire.

Aya 85:11

إِنَّ الَّذِينَ آمَنُوا وَعَمِلُوا الصَّالِحَاتِ لَهُمْ جَنَّاتٌ تَجْرِي مِن تَحْتِهَا الْأَنْهَارُ ذَٰلِكَ الْفَوْزُ الْكَبِيرُ

Surely, those who believed and did good deeds, for them are gardens (paradise), flowing from underneath it, are the rivers, that is the success, the big (great success).

Aya 85:12
إِنَّ بَطْشَ رَبِّكَ لَشَدِيدٌ

Surely, the attack (assault, punishment) of the Lord of yours (Allah) is definitely, intense (severe).

Aya 85:13
إِنَّهُ هُوَ يُبْدِئُ وَيُعِيدُ

Surely, He (Allah), He originates (begins the creation), and He (Allah) repeats (the creation by resurrection on the day of judgment).

Aya 85:14
وَهُوَ الْغَفُورُ الْوَدُودُ

And He (Allah) is the Most Forgiver, the Most Loving.

Aya 85:15
ذُو الْعَرْشِ الْمَجِيدُ

Owner of the Arsh (Throne of Allah), the Glorious.

Aya 85:16
فَعَّالٌ لِّمَا يُرِيدُ

The great doer of what He (Allah) intends (wants).

Aya 85:17
هَلْ أَتَاكَ حَدِيثُ الْجُنُودِ

Has come to you (O prophet Muhammad, peace be upon him), talk (story) of the armies?

Aya 85:18
فِرْعَوْنَ وَثَمُودَ

(armies of) Fir'aun and the (nation of) Thamud.

Aya 85:19

بَلِ الَّذِينَ كَفَرُوا فِي تَكْذِيبٍ

But, those who disbelieved are in belying (denying, rejecting the truth).

Aya 85:20

وَاللَّهُ مِن وَرَائِهِم مُّحِيطٌ

And Allah, from behind of theirs, is surrounding (encompassing).

Aya 85:21

بَلْ هُوَ قُرْآنٌ مَّجِيدٌ

But it is Quran, Glorious.

Aya 85:22

فِي لَوْحٍ مَّحْفُوظٍ

In the tablet preserved (Al-Lauh Al-Mahfuz is the written tablet or script of all knowledge with Allah).

سُورَةُ الطَّارِقِ

Sura Al Tariq

The Glorious Quran 86

بِسْمِ اللَّهِ الرَّحْمَٰنِ الرَّحِيمِ

(I begin) with the name of Allah, the Most Beneficent (Most Kind), the Most Merciful.

Aya 86:1
وَالسَّمَاءِ وَالطَّارِقِ

(Swear) By the sky (heaven) and by the Tariq (the bright star that appears at night or the night-comer).

Aya 86:2
وَمَا أَدْرَاكَ مَا الطَّارِقُ

And what made you understand, what is Tariq? (Night comer).

Aya 86:3
النَّجْمُ الثَّاقِبُ

The star, the piercer (having piercing brightness).

Aya 86:4
إِن كُلُّ نَفْسٍ لَّمَّا عَلَيْهَا حَافِظٌ

Not is all (every) self (person, soul), but on it (on that person, soul) is guardian (angel).

Aya 86:5
فَلْيَنظُرِ الْإِنسَانُ مِمَّ خُلِقَ

So should see the human from what was he (human) created.

Aya 86:6

خُلِقَ مِن مَّاءٍ دَافِقٍ

Created from water (semen) gushing.

Aya 86:7

يَخْرُجُ مِن بَيْنِ الصُّلْبِ وَالتَّرَائِبِ

(Water, semen) Coming out from in between the backbone and the ribs.

Aya 86:8

إِنَّهُ عَلَىٰ رَجْعِهِ لَقَادِرٌ

Surely, He (Allah) is on bringing back of his (of humans, bringing them back to life after death), is definitely, capable (powerful).

Aya 86:9

يَوْمَ تُبْلَى السَّرَائِرُ

On that day (of judgment), will be tested (examined or brought to open) (all) secrets.

Aya 86:10

فَمَا لَهُ مِن قُوَّةٍ وَلَا نَاصِرٍ

So, not is for him (for human) from (any) power, and not (is there for him, any) helper (on the day of judgment).

Aya 86:11

وَالسَّمَاءِ ذَاتِ الرَّجْعِ

By (swear) the sky with the return (giving rain again and again or revolving).

Aya 86:12

وَالْأَرْضِ ذَاتِ الصَّدْعِ

By (swear) the earth with the split (splits with plants).

Aya 86:13
إِنَّهُ لَقَوْلٌ فَصْلٌ

Surely, it (the Quran) is definitely the word decisive (discrete, that separates the truth from falsehood).

Aya 86:14
وَمَا هُوَ بِالْهَزْلِ

And not is it (the Quran) amusement (a joke).

Aya 86:15
إِنَّهُمْ يَكِيدُونَ كَيْدًا

Surely, they are plotting a plot (against the truth).

Aya 86:16
وَأَكِيدُ كَيْدًا

And I (Allah) make a plot (against their plot).

Aya 86:17
فَمَهِّلِ الْكَافِرِينَ أَمْهِلْهُمْ رُوَيْدًا

So, give delay (respite, time) to the disbelievers, give delay (respite, time) to them for a while.

سُوْرَةُ الْأَعْلَىٰ

Surat Al Aa'laa

The Glorious Quran 87

بِسْمِ اللَّهِ الرَّحْمَٰنِ الرَّحِيمِ

(I begin) with the name of Allah, the Most Beneficent (Most Kind), the Most Merciful.

Aya 87:1
سَبِّحِ اسْمَ رَبِّكَ الْأَعْلَى

Proclaim purity (glorify), for the name of Lord of yours (Allah), the Most High.

Aya 87:2
الَّذِي خَلَقَ فَسَوَّىٰ

The One (Allah) who created (everything), so proportioned (equaled, made everything what it was supposed to be).

Aya 87:3
وَالَّذِي قَدَّرَ فَهَدَىٰ

And the One (Allah) who destined (determined, ordained), so guided.

Aya 87:4
وَالَّذِي أَخْرَجَ الْمَرْعَىٰ

And the One (Allah) who brought out the pasturage (greenery).

Aya 87:5
فَجَعَلَهُ غُثَاءً أَحْوَىٰ

So made it (the greenery) stubble (dried up left over), dark (dust-colored).

Aya 87:6

سَنُقْرِئُكَ فَلَا تَنسَىٰ

Soon, We (Allah) will make you (O prophet Muhammad, peace be upon him) recite (the Quran), So not you will forget.

Aya 87:7

إِلَّا مَا شَاءَ اللَّهُ إِنَّهُ يَعْلَمُ الْجَهْرَ وَمَا يَخْفَىٰ

Except for what wanted (willed) Allah, surely, He (Allah) knows the loud (speech) and what is hidden.

Aya 87:8

وَنُيَسِّرُكَ لِلْيُسْرَىٰ

And We (Allah) will ease you (O prophet Muhammad, peace be upon him) for easiness.
(Make your way easy to the state of easiness.)

Aya 87:9

فَذَكِّرْ إِن نَّفَعَتِ الذِّكْرَىٰ

Therefore, remind (advise people) if (or surely) profits the reminder.
 (if the reminder will be heard and understood.)

Aya 87:10

سَيَذَّكَّرُ مَن يَخْشَىٰ

Soon, will remember (will accept the reminder and believe) the one who fears (Allah).

Aya 87:11

وَيَتَجَنَّبُهَا الْأَشْقَى

And will avoid it (reject the remembrance and the advice)
the most unfortunate (wretched).

Aya 87:12

الَّذِي يَصْلَى النَّارَ الْكُبْرَىٰ

The one (wretched person) who will reach (enter) the fire, the big (fire).

Aya 87:13

ثُمَّ لَا يَمُوتُ فِيهَا وَلَا يَحْيَىٰ

Then, not will he die in it (in hellfire) and not will he live (will neither die nor live therein).

Aya 87:14

قَدْ أَفْلَحَ مَن تَزَكَّىٰ

Surely, succeeded the one who purified (the self from impurities of polytheism and bad deeds).

Aya 87:15

وَذَكَرَ اسْمَ رَبِّهِ فَصَلَّىٰ

And remembered (zikr) the name of Lord of his (Allah) and so he prayed.

Aya 87:16

بَلْ تُؤْثِرُونَ الْحَيَاةَ الدُّنْيَا

But you (all) prefer the life of the world.

Aya 87:17

وَالْآخِرَةُ خَيْرٌ وَأَبْقَىٰ

And the hereafter is better and more lasting.

Aya 87:18

إِنَّ هَٰذَا لَفِي الصُّحُفِ الْأُولَىٰ

Surely, this (message) is, in the scriptures, the earlier (books of Allah).

Aya 87:19

صُحُفِ إِبْرَاهِيمَ وَمُوسَىٰ

The Scriptures of (prophet) Ibraheem and (book of prophet) Musa (peace be upon both of them).

سُورَةُ الْغَاشِيَةِ

Surat Al Ghaashiah

The Glorious Quran 88

بِسْمِ اللَّهِ الرَّحْمَٰنِ الرَّحِيمِ

(I begin) with the name of Allah, the Most Beneficent (Most Kind), the Most Merciful.

Aya 88:1

هَلْ أَتَاكَ حَدِيثُ الْغَاشِيَةِ

Has come to you (O prophet Muhammad, peace be upon him) the talk (narration) of the covering one (the overwhelming day of Resurrection).

Aya 88:2

وُجُوهٌ يَوْمَئِذٍ خَاشِعَةٌ

(Some) Faces on that day, (will be) humbled (humiliated).

Aya 88:3

عَامِلَةٌ نَّاصِبَةٌ

Laboring, exhausted.

Aya 88:4

تَصْلَىٰ نَارًا حَامِيَةً

Will reach the fire, hot (blazing)

Aya 88:5

تُسْقَىٰ مِنْ عَيْنٍ آنِيَةٍ

(Will be) given to drink from spring, boiling.

Aya 88:6
لَّيْسَ لَهُمْ طَعَامٌ إِلَّا مِن ضَرِيعٍ

Not, is for them, food, except Dhareegh (a bitter thorny plant in the hell).

Aya 88:7
لَّا يُسْمِنُ وَلَا يُغْنِي مِن جُوعٍ

Not it (that food from Dhareegh) nourishes and not it gives benefit (freedom, avail) from hunger.

Aya 88:8
وُجُوهٌ يَوْمَئِذٍ نَّاعِمَةٌ

(Other) Faces, that day, will be blissful (joyful, fresh and shining).

Aya 88:9
لِّسَعْيِهَا رَاضِيَةٌ

For efforts of it (for their good deeds in the worldly life) satisfied (well pleased).

Aya 88:10
فِي جَنَّةٍ عَالِيَةٍ

In gardens (that are) high (lofty and superior).

Aya 88:11
لَّا تَسْمَعُ فِيهَا لَاغِيَةً

Not will they (residents of paradise) hear in it (in paradise) useless talk.

Aya 88:12
فِيهَا عَيْنٌ جَارِيَةٌ

In it (in paradise) is fountain flowing.

Aya 88:13
فِيهَا سُرُرٌ مَّرْفُوعَةٌ

In it (in paradise) are couches (thrones) raised high.

Aya 88:14

وَأَكْوَابٌ مَّوْضُوعَةٌ

And (in paradise are) cups placed (set at hand).

Aya 88:15

وَنَمَارِقُ مَصْفُوفَةٌ

And (in paradise are) cushions set in rows (lined up).

Aya 88:16

وَزَرَابِيُّ مَبْثُوثَةٌ

And (in paradise are) carpets spread out.

Aya 88:17

أَفَلَا يَنظُرُونَ إِلَى الْإِبِلِ كَيْفَ خُلِقَتْ

Do not, they look at the camels, how are they (camels) created?

Aya 88:18

وَإِلَى السَّمَاءِ كَيْفَ رُفِعَتْ

And (do not, they look) at the sky, how was it (the sky) raised high?

Aya 88:19

وَإِلَى الْجِبَالِ كَيْفَ نُصِبَتْ

And (do not they look) at the mountains, how are they (mountains) set up (erected, installed, fixed, rooted)?

Aya 88:20

وَإِلَى الْأَرْضِ كَيْفَ سُطِحَتْ

And (do not they look) at the earth, how is it (the earth) leveled (spread out)?

Aya 88:21

فَذَكِّرْ إِنَّمَا أَنتَ مُذَكِّرٌ

So remind them (tell them the right path, O Prophet Muhammad, peace be upon him), surely that you (O Prophet Muhammad, peace be upon him) are the reminder (to give advice and remembrance).

Aya 88:22

لَّسْتَ عَلَيْهِم بِمُصَيْطِرٍ

Not are you (O prophet Muhammad, peace be upon him) over them, a controller (compeller).

Aya 88:23

إِلَّا مَن تَوَلَّىٰ وَكَفَرَ

Except the one who turned away and disbelieved (rejected the message).

Aya 88:24

فَيُعَذِّبُهُ اللَّهُ الْعَذَابَ الْأَكْبَرَ

So, punish will him, Allah, the punishment, the greatest (punishment)

Aya 88:25

إِنَّ إِلَيْنَا إِيَابَهُمْ

Surely, toward Us (Allah), is coming back (return) of theirs.

Aya 88:26

ثُمَّ إِنَّ عَلَيْنَا حِسَابَهُم

Then, surely, on Us (on Allah) is accounts of theirs (accounts of good and bad deeds).

سُورَةُ الفَجْرِ

Surat Al Fajr

The Glorious Quran 89

بِسْمِ اللَّهِ الرَّحْمَٰنِ الرَّحِيمِ

(I begin) with the name of Allah, the Most Beneficent (Most Kind), the Most Merciful.

Aya 89:1

وَالْفَجْرِ

(I Swear) by the dawn (daybreak).

Aya 89:2

وَلَيَالٍ عَشْرٍ

And (I swear) by the nights ten (first ten nights of the month of Dhul Hijja).

Aya 89:3

وَالشَّفْعِ وَالْوَتْرِ

And I (swear) by the even and the odd.

Aya 89:4

وَاللَّيْلِ إِذَا يَسْرِ

And (I swear) by the night when it passes (departs).

Aya 89:5

هَلْ فِي ذَٰلِكَ قَسَمٌ لِّذِي حِجْرٍ

Is there, in that, (in swearing above) oath (enough swearing) for the owner of intelligence (understanding)?

Aya 89:6

أَلَمْ تَرَ كَيْفَ فَعَلَ رَبُّكَ بِعَادٍ

Did not you see, how did (dealt) Lord of yours (Allah) with (nation of) 'A'ad?

Aya 89:7
إِرَمَ ذَاتِ الْعِمَادِ

(The people of) Iram, owner of the pillars (lofty buildings).

Aya 89:8
الَّتِي لَمْ يُخْلَقْ مِثْلُهَا فِي الْبِلَادِ

The one, none was created like it (like the nation of A'ad), in the towns (in lands).

Aya 89:9
وَثَمُودَ الَّذِينَ جَابُوا الصَّخْرَ بِالْوَادِ

And (nation of) Thamud, those that carved out the rocks in the valley.

Aya 89:10
وَفِرْعَوْنَ ذِي الْأَوْتَادِ

And Fir'aun, owner of the (tent) pegs (stakes, or owner of the power).

Aya 89:11
الَّذِينَ طَغَوْا فِي الْبِلَادِ

Those (people) who transgressed (rebelled) in the towns (in lands).

Aya 89:12
فَأَكْثَرُوا فِيهَا الْفَسَادَ

And they increased (did much more) in it (in cities and lands) the corruption (mischief).

Aya 89:13
فَصَبَّ عَلَيْهِمْ رَبُّكَ سَوْطَ عَذَابٍ

So poured upon them (on those transgressors), Lord of yours (Allah), the whip of punishment.

Aya 89:14

إِنَّ رَبَّكَ لَبِالْمِرْصَادِ

Surely, the Lord of yours (Allah) is definitely on the watch (watchful).

Aya 89:15

فَأَمَّا الْإِنسَانُ إِذَا مَا ابْتَلَاهُ رَبُّهُ فَأَكْرَمَهُ وَنَعَّمَهُ فَيَقُولُ رَبِّي أَكْرَمَنِ

So as for human, whenever tried him (human), Lord of his (Allah), so honored him (the human) and gifted him (the human with bounties and giving), so he (the human) says, the Lord of mine (Allah) has honored me.
(Considers worldly wealth and honor as a sign of approval by Allah, which is not a must).

Aya 89:16

وَأَمَّا إِذَا مَا ابْتَلَاهُ فَقَدَرَ عَلَيْهِ رِزْقَهُ فَيَقُولُ رَبِّي أَهَانَنِ

And whenever He (Allah) tried him (the human), so measured (restricted) on him (on human) sustenance (food and wealth) of his, so he (the human) says, the Lord of mine (Allah) has humiliated me.
(Considers worldly restrictions in wealth and food as a sign of disapproval by Allah, which is not a must).

Aya 89:17

كَلَّا بَل لَّا تُكْرِمُونَ الْيَتِيمَ

Nay (no, no, but) but not, you honor (you do not respect and take care of) the orphan.

Aya 89:18

وَلَا تَحَاضُّونَ عَلَىٰ طَعَامِ الْمِسْكِينِ

And not you urge (not you encourage one another) on feeding the poor.

Aya 89:19

وَتَأْكُلُونَ التُّرَاثَ أَكْلًا لَّمًّا

And you eat the inheritance, eating of the greed (gulping, eating indiscriminately).

Aya 89:20

وَتُحِبُّونَ الْمَالَ حُبًّا جَمًّا

And you love the wealth, love intense (extreme love).

Aya 89:21

كَلَّا إِذَا دُكَّتِ الْأَرْضُ دَكًّا دَكًّا

Nay (no, no but), when crushed, will be the earth, with crushing (upon) crushing.

Aya 89:22

وَجَاءَ رَبُّكَ وَالْمَلَكُ صَفًّا صَفًّا

And came the Lord of yours (Allah) and angels standing row (on) row.

Aya 89:23

وَجِيءَ يَوْمَئِذٍ بِجَهَنَّمَ يَوْمَئِذٍ يَتَذَكَّرُ الْإِنْسَانُ وَأَنَّىٰ لَهُ الذِّكْرَىٰ

And brought (in) is that day (of judgment), the hell (near and upfront), on that day (of judgment) will remember (realize) the human and from where will be, for him (the human) the remembrance (how will it benefit him, on that day of judgment).

Aya 89:24

يَقُولُ يَا لَيْتَنِي قَدَّمْتُ لِحَيَاتِي

He (human) will say, Oh, I wish that I had sent forward (some good deeds) for the life of mine (this real life of hereafter).

Aya 89:25

فَيَوْمَئِذٍ لَا يُعَذِّبُ عَذَابَهُ أَحَدٌ

So, that Day (of judgment) not will punish, (like) punishment of His (Allah), anyone.

Aya 89:26

وَلَا يُوثِقُ وَثَاقَهُ أَحَدٌ

And not will bind (in chains like) binding of His (Allah) anyone.

Aya 89:27

يَا أَيَّتُهَا النَّفْسُ الْمُطْمَئِنَّةُ

(Allah will say), O you, the nafs (person) satisfied (pious person with eman and good deeds).

Aya 89:28

ارْجِعِي إِلَىٰ رَبِّكِ رَاضِيَةً مَّرْضِيَّةً

Come back to Lord of yours (Allah), well-pleased and well-pleasing.

Aya 89:29

فَادْخُلِي فِي عِبَادِي

So, you enter (amongst pious) servants of Mine (servants of Allah).

Aya 89:30

وَادْخُلِي جَنَّتِي

And you enter the garden of Mine (Allah's paradise).

سُورَةُ الْبَلَدِ

Surat Al Balad

The Glorious Quran 90

بِسْمِ اللَّهِ الرَّحْمَٰنِ الرَّحِيمِ

(I begin) with the name of Allah, the Most Beneficent (Most Kind), the Most Merciful.

Aya 90:1
لَا أُقْسِمُ بِهَٰذَا الْبَلَدِ

No (no, no, but) I (Allah) swear by this city (of Makkah).

Aya 90:2
وَأَنتَ حِلٌّ بِهَٰذَا الْبَلَدِ

And you (O Prophet Muhammad, peace be upon him) are allowed (halal for you to fight back the enemy, you are free, or you are a dweller) in this city (of Makkah).

Aya 90:3
وَوَالِدٍ وَمَا وَلَدَ

And (I swear by) the father and what he begot (what was born to him).

Aya 90:4
لَقَدْ خَلَقْنَا الْإِنسَانَ فِي كَبَدٍ

Surely, We (Allah) created the human in struggle (in hardship and distress).

Aya 90:5
أَيَحْسَبُ أَن لَّن يَقْدِرَ عَلَيْهِ أَحَدٌ

Does he suppose (thinks) that never will overpower (prevail) on him anyone?

Aya 90:6
يَقُولُ أَهْلَكْتُ مَالًا لُبَدًا

He (the human) says I have spent wealth in abundance.

Aya 90:7
أَيَحْسَبُ أَن لَّمْ يَرَهُ أَحَدٌ

Does he suppose (thinks) that not will see him anyone?

Aya 90:8
أَلَمْ نَجْعَل لَّهُ عَيْنَيْنِ

Have not We (Allah) made for him two eyes?

Aya 90:9
وَلِسَانًا وَشَفَتَيْنِ

And (a) tongue and two lips?

Aya 90:10
وَهَدَيْنَاهُ النَّجْدَيْنِ

And We (Allah) guided (showed) him (the human), the two ways (good and evil)?

Aya 90:11
فَلَا اقْتَحَمَ الْعَقَبَةَ

So not has he tried the hardship of the steep rise (of the difficult and hard path) (He has not tried the difficult and steep path of spending in the path of Allah without showing off).

Aya 90:12
وَمَا أَدْرَاكَ مَا الْعَقَبَةُ

And what made you know what is the steep rise (of the difficult path)?

Aya 90:13
فَكُّ رَقَبَةٍ

(That difficult path is) Freeing (a) neck (to free a slave).

Aya 90:14
أَوْ إِطْعَامٌ فِي يَوْمٍ ذِي مَسْغَبَةٍ

(That difficult path is) Or feeding in a day, owner of starvation (the day with hunger and famine).

Aya 90:15
يَتِيمًا ذَا مَقْرَبَةٍ

(Feeding) an orphan owner of (a) relationship (an orphan who is your relative).

Aya 90:16
أَوْ مِسْكِينًا ذَا مَتْرَبَةٍ

Or (to feed) a poor person owner of dust (dusty poor person).

Aya 90:17
ثُمَّ كَانَ مِنَ الَّذِينَ آمَنُوا وَتَوَاصَوْا بِالصَّبْرِ وَتَوَاصَوْا بِالْمَرْحَمَةِ

Then, (that person on the difficult and true path of charity) he was (joined others) from those people who believed (joined the group of other believers) and advised (counsel others) with patience and advised (counseled others) with mercy (compassion).

Aya 90:18
أُولَٰئِكَ أَصْحَابُ الْمَيْمَنَةِ

Those (who crossed this steep path) are the people of the right (people of paradise).

Aya 90:19
وَالَّذِينَ كَفَرُوا بِآيَاتِنَا هُمْ أَصْحَابُ الْمَشْأَمَةِ

And those who disbelieved in signs (verses) of Ours (Allah), they are companions of the left (people of Hell).

Aya 90:20
عَلَيْهِمْ نَارٌ مُّؤْصَدَةٌ

On them (people of left) will be fire closed in (vaulted, enclosed, they will be enveloped by the fire, closed in, without any opening or outlet to escape).

سُورَةُ الشَّمْسِ

Surat Al Shams

The Glorious Quran 91

بِسْمِ اللَّهِ الرَّحْمَٰنِ الرَّحِيمِ

(I begin) with the name of Allah, the Most Beneficent (Most Kind), the Most Merciful.

Aya 91:1
وَالشَّمْسِ وَضُحَاهَا

(I swear) By the sun and light of it (brilliance of the sun).

Aya 91:2
وَالْقَمَرِ إِذَا تَلَاهَا

And (I swear) by the moon when it follows (adjoins) it (the sun).

Aya 91:3
وَالنَّهَارِ إِذَا جَلَّاهَا

And (I swear) by the day when it displays (brightens) it (the sun).

Aya 91:4
وَاللَّيْلِ إِذَا يَغْشَاهَا

And (I swear) by the night when it covers (conceals) it (the sun).

Aya 91:5
وَالسَّمَاءِ وَمَا بَنَاهَا

And (I swear) by the sky (heaven) and what He (Allah) built it (sky).

Aya 91:6
وَالْأَرْضِ وَمَا طَحَاهَا

And (I swear) by the earth and what He (Allah) spread it (the earth).

Aya 91:7
وَنَفْسٍ وَمَا سَوَّاهَا

And (I swear) by the Nafs (human person) and what He (Allah) equaled (perfected, proportioned) it (the nafs, person).

Aya 91:8
فَأَلْهَمَهَا فُجُورَهَا وَتَقْوَاهَا

So, He (Allah) inspired (revealed, showed) to it (to the nafs) sin of it and piety of it (wrong and guided ways).

Aya 91:9
قَدْ أَفْلَحَ مَن زَكَّاهَا

Surely, succeeded the one, who purified it (the nafs, who cleaned and purified himself)

Aya 91:10
وَقَدْ خَابَ مَن دَسَّاهَا

And surely, failed (got disappointed) the one, who corrupted it (corrupted his nafs, corrupted his own self)
(the world "Dassaha", means corrupted, stunted, polluted)

Aya 91:11
كَذَّبَتْ ثَمُودُ بِطَغْوَاهَا

Belied (rejected the message of Allah, the nation of) Thamud, on transgression of it (rejected Allah due to their transgression).

Aya 91:12
إِذِ انبَعَثَ أَشْقَاهَا

When it (the people of Thamud) sent (or arose) the most wicked of it (they sent the most wicked person amongst them to kill the she-camel).

Aya 91:13
فَقَالَ لَهُمْ رَسُولُ اللَّهِ نَاقَةَ اللَّهِ وَسُقْيَاهَا

So, said for them (was said to the people of Thamud by the) messenger of Allah (peace be upon him), (this is the) she-camel of Allah and (should have a turn of) drinking of it (let her drink water).

Aya 91:14
فَكَذَّبُوهُ فَعَقَرُوهَا فَدَمْدَمَ عَلَيْهِمْ رَبُّهُم بِذَنبِهِمْ فَسَوَّاهَا

So, they belied (rejected) him (the messenger, peace be upon him), and they hamstrung her (and later killed the she-camel), so sent devastating punishment on them, Lord of theirs (Allah), on (due to) sin of theirs, so He (Allah) equaled (levelled) it (destroyed the nation of Thamud).

Aya 91:15
وَلَا يَخَافُ عُقْبَاهَا

And not, He (Allah) fears the consequences of it (the consequence of their destruction).

سُورَةُ اللَّيْلِ

Surat Al Lail

The Glorious Quran 92

بِسْمِ اللَّهِ الرَّحْمَٰنِ الرَّحِيمِ

(I begin) with the name of Allah, the Most Beneficent (Most Kind), the Most Merciful.

Aya 92:1
وَاللَّيْلِ إِذَا يَغْشَىٰ

(I swear) By the night, when it covers (everything with darkness).

Aya 92:2
وَالنَّهَارِ إِذَا تَجَلَّىٰ

And (swear) by the day when it brightens (everything with light).

Aya 92:3
وَمَا خَلَقَ الذَّكَرَ وَالْأُنثَىٰ

And (swear) by what He (Allah) created, the male and the female.

Aya 92:4
إِنَّ سَعْيَكُمْ لَشَتَّىٰ

Surely, efforts of yours, definitely, are scattered (diverse and different in aims and purposes).

Aya 92:5
فَأَمَّا مَنْ أَعْطَىٰ وَاتَّقَىٰ

As for the one, who gave (to the poor in charity) and practiced piety (avoided sins for the fear of Allah).

Aya 92:6
وَصَدَّقَ بِالْحُسْنَىٰ

And pronounced as truth (confirmed, testified), on the best (religion of Allah).

Aya 92:7
فَسَنُيَسِّرُهُ لِلْيُسْرَىٰ

So, soon, We (Allah) will ease him (the true believer) for the easiness (of goodness and easiness of paradise).

Aya 92:8
وَأَمَّا مَن بَخِلَ وَاسْتَغْنَىٰ

And as for the one, who practiced misery (stinginess by hoarding money) and acted self-sufficiently (did not care).

Aya 92:9
وَكَذَّبَ بِالْحُسْنَىٰ

And belied (rejected) on the best (religion of Islam).

Aya 92:10
فَسَنُيَسِّرُهُ لِلْعُسْرَىٰ

So, soon, We (Allah) will ease him (the rejector) for hardship (the difficult end here and in the hereafter).

Aya 92:11
وَمَا يُغْنِي عَنْهُ مَالُهُ إِذَا تَرَدَّىٰ

And not will save (benefit, avail) from him (from the rejector) wealth of his (from the punishment of Allah), when he falls (topples into hellfire or die).

Aya 92:12
إِنَّ عَلَيْنَا لَلْهُدَىٰ

Surely, on Us (Allah) is the (giving of) guidance.

Aya 92:13
وَإِنَّ لَنَا لَلْآخِرَةَ وَالْأُولَىٰ

And surely for Us (only to Allah belongs) the Hereafter (life after death) and the earlier (life in this world).

Aya 92:14
فَأَنذَرْتُكُمْ نَارًا تَلَظَّىٰ

So, I warned you of a fire, that blazes fiercely.

Aya 92:15
لَا يَصْلَاهَا إِلَّا الْأَشْقَى

Not will reach (enter) it (the fire), except the unlucky one (the wretched, the wicked).

Aya 92:16
الَّذِي كَذَّبَ وَتَوَلَّىٰ

The one (wicked one) who belied (rejected the true religion) and turned away (from Allah).

Aya 92:17
وَسَيُجَنَّبُهَا الْأَتْقَى

And soon, will be kept away (saved) from it (from the blazing fire) the most pious (righteous) one.
 (Pious-who avoid bad deeds for the fear of Allah)

Aya 92:18
الَّذِي يُؤْتِي مَالَهُ يَتَزَكَّىٰ

The one (pious person) who gives (spends) wealth of his, purifying (himself from sins).

Aya 92:19
وَمَا لِأَحَدٍ عِندَهُ مِن نِّعْمَةٍ تُجْزَىٰ

And not (is there), for (any) one (person) with him, from (any) favor being rewarded (being returned).
(Spends his wealth for the sake of Allah, without obligation to anyone, not for the purpose of returning favor for someone).

Aya 92:20
إِلَّا ابْتِغَاءَ وَجْهِ رَبِّهِ الْأَعْلَىٰ

(Not spending his wealth) Except (for) seeking the Face (pleasure) of the Lord of his (Allah), the Most High.

Aya 92:21
وَلَسَوْفَ يَرْضَىٰ

And definitely, soon, he will please (will be happy). (The pious person will be pleased and happy in paradise, or Allah will be pleased with him)

سُورَةُ الضُّحَىٰ

Surat Al Duha

The Glorious Quran 93

بِسْمِ اللهِ الرَّحْمَٰنِ الرَّحِيمِ

(I begin) with the name of Allah, the Most Beneficent (Most Kind), the Most Merciful.

Aya 93:1
وَالضُّحَىٰ

(I swear) By the forenoon (morning brightness).

Aya 93:2
وَاللَّيْلِ إِذَا سَجَىٰ

And (swear) by the night when it (the night) darkened (became settled and still with darkness).

Aya 93:3
مَا وَدَّعَكَ رَبُّكَ وَمَا قَلَىٰ

Not abandoned you (O Prophet Muhammad, peace be upon him, by) Lord of yours (Allah), and not is He (Allah) displeased (with you).

Aya 93:4
وَلَلْآخِرَةُ خَيْرٌ لَكَ مِنَ الْأُولَىٰ

And surely, the later (time, what comes after or hereafter) is better for you from (as compared to) the earlier (time that has gone before or the worldly life).

Aya 93:5
وَلَسَوْفَ يُعْطِيكَ رَبُّكَ فَتَرْضَىٰ

And soon, will give you, Lord of yours (Allah) so you are pleased.

Aya 93:6
أَلَمْ يَجِدْكَ يَتِيمًا فَآوَىٰ

Did not He (Allah) find you (O prophet Muhammad, peace be upon him) (an) orphan, and He (Allah) gave you a place (shelter)?

Aya 93:7
وَوَجَدَكَ ضَالًّا فَهَدَىٰ

And He (Allah) found you lost (unaware), so He (Allah) guided (you).

Aya 93:8
وَوَجَدَكَ عَائِلًا فَأَغْنَىٰ

And He (Allah) found you poor, so He (Allah) made you self-sufficient (carefree).

Aya 93:9
فَأَمَّا الْيَتِيمَ فَلَا تَقْهَرْ

So, as far as the orphan, so not you treat (him) with anger (do not treat orphans with harshness).

Aya 93:10
وَأَمَّا السَّائِلَ فَلَا تَنْهَرْ

And as far as the asker (any person asking for money or favor, beggar), so not you repulse (scold, treat harshly)

Aya 93:11
وَأَمَّا بِنِعْمَةِ رَبِّكَ فَحَدِّثْ

And as far as on giving (bounty, grace) of the Lord of yours (Allah), so you do talk (mention and proclaim).

سُوْرَةُ الْإِنْشِرَاحِ

Surat Al Inshirah

The Glorious Quran 94

بِسْمِ اللَّهِ الرَّحْمَٰنِ الرَّحِيمِ

(I begin) with the name of Allah, the Most Beneficent (Most Kind), the Most Merciful.

Aya 94:1
أَلَمْ نَشْرَحْ لَكَ صَدْرَكَ

Did not We (Allah) open (expanded) for you (O prophet Muhammad, peace be upon him) chest of yours?

Aya 94:2
وَوَضَعْنَا عَنكَ وِزْرَكَ

And We (Allah) removed from you (O prophet Muhammad, peace be upon him) burden of yours?

Aya 94:3
الَّذِي أَنقَضَ ظَهْرَكَ

The one (burden, stress) that broke back of yours?

Aya 94:4
وَرَفَعْنَا لَكَ ذِكْرَكَ

And We (Allah) raised for you (O Prophet Muhammad, peace be upon him) remembrance of yours (reputation, fame).

Aya 94:5
فَإِنَّ مَعَ الْعُسْرِ يُسْرًا

So surely, with the hardship is the ease (relief).

Aya 94:6
إِنَّ مَعَ الْعُسْرِ يُسْرًا

Surely, with the hardship is the ease (relief).
(With one hardship, there are two reliefs, so one hardship cannot overcome two reliefs).

Aya 94:7
فَإِذَا فَرَغْتَ فَانصَبْ

So, when you become free (done with your duties), exert yourself hard (fatigue yourself, labor hard by standing up in prayers for Allah).

Aya 94:8
وَإِلَىٰ رَبِّكَ فَارْغَب

And toward Lord of yours (Allah), so you turn, in eagerness (with love and hope).

سُوْرَة التين

Surat Al Theen

The Glorious Quran 95

بِسْمِ اللَّهِ الرَّحْمَٰنِ الرَّحِيمِ

(I begin) with the name of Allah, the Most Beneficent (Most Kind), the Most Merciful.

Aya 95:1
وَالتِّينِ وَالزَّيْتُونِ

(I swear) By the fig and the olive.

Aya 95:2
وَطُورِ سِينِينَ

And (I swear by mountain) Toor of Sineen (Mountain of Sinai)

Aya 95:3
وَهَٰذَا الْبَلَدِ الْأَمِينِ

And (I swear by) this city, the secure (peaceful city of Makkah).

Aya 95:4
لَقَدْ خَلَقْنَا الْإِنسَانَ فِي أَحْسَنِ تَقْوِيمٍ

Surely, We (Allah) created the human in the best stature (best standing, upright, best moulding).

Aya 95:5
ثُمَّ رَدَدْنَاهُ أَسْفَلَ سَافِلِينَ

Then We (Allah) returned (rendered or reduced) him to the lowest of the low (s) (the lowest form of the weakness in old age, lowest in morality, or sent to the lowest part of the hell).

Aya 95:6

إِلَّا الَّذِينَ آمَنُوا وَعَمِلُوا الصَّالِحَاتِ فَلَهُمْ أَجْرٌ غَيْرُ مَمْنُونٍ

Except those who believed and did the good deeds so, for them, is the reward never-ending (not failing).

Aya 95:7

فَمَا يُكَذِّبُكَ بَعْدُ بِالدِّينِ

So, what makes you (O human) belie (to reject) after (this reminder), on the deen (the religion or the day of judgment)?

Aya 95:8

أَلَيْسَ اللَّهُ بِأَحْكَمِ الْحَاكِمِينَ

Is not Allah the Best Ruler (or Best Judge) of all the rulers (or judges)?

سُورَةُ العَلَقِ

Surat Al A'laq

The Glorious Quran 96

بِسْمِ اللَّهِ الرَّحْمَٰنِ الرَّحِيمِ

(I begin) with the name of Allah, the Most Beneficent (Most Kind), the Most Merciful.

Aya 96:1
اقْرَأْ بِاسْمِ رَبِّكَ الَّذِي خَلَقَ

Read with the name of Lord of yours (Allah), the one who created (everything).

Aya 96:2
خَلَقَ الْإِنسَانَ مِنْ عَلَقٍ

He (Allah) created the human from (a) clot (clinging substance).

Aya 96:3
اقْرَأْ وَرَبُّكَ الْأَكْرَمُ

Read, and Lord of yours (Allah) is the Most Generous (Noble, Honorable).

Aya 96:4
الَّذِي عَلَّمَ بِالْقَلَمِ

The One (Allah) who taught (everyone to write) with (a) pen.

Aya 96:5
عَلَّمَ الْإِنسَانَ مَا لَمْ يَعْلَمْ

He (Allah) taught the human what, not he knew.

Aya 96:6
كَلَّا إِنَّ الْإِنسَانَ لَيَطْغَىٰ

Nay (no, no, but), surely the human, definitely, transgresses (rebels, crosses limits).

Aya 96:7
أَن رَّآهُ اسْتَغْنَىٰ

That, he (human) saw himself, becoming self-sufficient (free of needs).

Aya 96:8
إِنَّ إِلَىٰ رَبِّكَ الرُّجْعَىٰ

Surely, toward the Lord of yours (Allah) is the return (going back).

Aya 96:9
أَرَأَيْتَ الَّذِي يَنْهَىٰ

Did you (O prophet Muhammad, peace be upon him) see the one who forbids (prevents, stops, meaning Abu Jahl stopping prophet Muhammad, peace be upon him, from praying)?

Aya 96:10
عَبْدًا إِذَا صَلَّىٰ

(Forbids the) Servant (of Allah, meaning, prophet (Muhammad Peace be upon him)) when he prayed?

Aya 96:11
أَرَأَيْتَ إِن كَانَ عَلَى الْهُدَىٰ

Did you see if he was on the guidance (right path)?

Aya 96:12
أَوْ أَمَرَ بِالتَّقْوَىٰ

Or he ordered (others) on taqwa (piety, avoiding sins for the fear of Allah).

Aya 96:13
أَرَأَيْتَ إِن كَذَّبَ وَتَوَلَّىٰ

Did you see if he belied (rejected Quran) and turned away (from the guidance)?

Aya 96:14
أَلَمْ يَعْلَم بِأَنَّ اللَّهَ يَرَىٰ

Not, he knows that Allah sees (what he is doing)?

Aya 96:15
كَلَّا لَئِن لَّمْ يَنتَهِ لَنَسْفَعًا بِالنَّاصِيَةِ

Nay (no, no but), if not, he stops (ceases), definitely, We (Allah) will catch him by the forelock.

Aya 96:16
نَاصِيَةٍ كَاذِبَةٍ خَاطِئَةٍ

Forelock liar, wrongful (sinful forelock).

Aya 96:17
فَلْيَدْعُ نَادِيَهُ

So, he (Abu Jahal) to call upon (invoke the help of) assembly (associates and friends of Abu Jahl) of his

Aya 96:18
سَنَدْعُ الزَّبَانِيَةَ

Soon, We (Allah) will call the Zabaniya (guards of Hell).

Aya 96:19
كَلَّا لَا تُطِعْهُ وَاسْجُدْ وَاقْتَرِب

Nay (no, no but), not you (O Muhammad peace be upon him) obey him (Abu Jahl) and (you) do Sajda (prostrate) and (you) get near (get close to Allah by worship and obedience).
(This is ayat of sajda, please do sajda now).

سُورَةُ القَدْرِ

Surat Al Qadr

The Glorious Quran 97

بِسْمِ اللَّهِ الرَّحْمَٰنِ الرَّحِيمِ

(I begin) with the name of Allah, the Most Beneficent (Most Kind), the Most Merciful.

Aya 97:1
إِنَّا أَنزَلْنَاهُ فِي لَيْلَةِ الْقَدْرِ

Surely, We (Allah) revealed (sent down) it (this Quran), in the night of the Al-Qadr (Night of determination, night of decree, night of power, night of predestination).

Aya 97:2
وَمَا أَدْرَاكَ مَا لَيْلَةُ الْقَدْرِ

And what made you know (understand) what the night of Al-Qadr is?

Aya 97:3
لَيْلَةُ الْقَدْرِ خَيْرٌ مِّنْ أَلْفِ شَهْرٍ

The night of Al-Qadr is better from (than a) thousand months.

Aya 97:4
تَنَزَّلُ الْمَلَائِكَةُ وَالرُّوحُ فِيهَا بِإِذْنِ رَبِّهِم مِّن كُلِّ أَمْرٍ

Descend the angels and the Ruh (Angle Jib'raeel) in it (in Lailt ul Qadr) with permission of the Lord of theirs (Allah), from (with commands and decrees for) all issues (all affairs, all kinds of decrees).

Aya 97:5
سَلَامٌ هِيَ حَتَّىٰ مَطْلَعِ الْفَجْرِ

(Full of) peace, this (night of Al-Qadr), is till the rise (appearance) of the Fajr (dawn, morning).

سُورَةُ البَيِّنَةِ

Surat Al Bayyina

The Glorious Quran 98

بِسْمِ اللَّهِ الرَّحْمَٰنِ الرَّحِيمِ

(I begin) with the name of Allah, the Most Beneficent (Most Kind), the Most Merciful.

Aya 98.1

لَمْ يَكُنِ الَّذِينَ كَفَرُوا مِنْ أَهْلِ الْكِتَابِ وَالْمُشْرِكِينَ مُنفَكِّينَ حَتَّىٰ تَأْتِيَهُمُ الْبَيِّنَةُ

Not are those who disbelieved (rejected), from the people of the book and (from) the polytheists (infidels of Makkah), stoppers (to cease and desist from their disbelief), till comes to them clear evidence.

Aya 98.2

رَسُولٌ مِّنَ اللَّهِ يَتْلُو صُحُفًا مُّطَهَّرَةً

(That clear evidence is) Messenger (peace be upon him) from Allah, reciting manuscripts (scroll) purified (by Allah from all defects).

Aya 98.3

فِيهَا كُتُبٌ قَيِّمَةٌ

In it (in that manuscript) are books upright (straight, strong, established evidences).

Aya 98.4

وَمَا تَفَرَّقَ الَّذِينَ أُوتُوا الْكِتَابَ إِلَّا مِنْ بَعْدِ مَا جَاءَتْهُمُ الْبَيِّنَةُ

And not divided (disagreed and disunited in sects) those people who were given the book (Jews and Christians) except after that came to them (the people of the book), the clear evidence.

Aya 98:5

وَمَآ أُمِرُوٓا۟ إِلَّا لِيَعْبُدُوا۟ ٱللَّهَ مُخْلِصِينَ لَهُ ٱلدِّينَ حُنَفَآءَ وَيُقِيمُوا۟ ٱلصَّلَوٰةَ وَيُؤْتُوا۟ ٱلزَّكَوٰةَ ۚ وَذَٰلِكَ دِينُ ٱلْقَيِّمَةِ

And not, were they (the people of the book) ordered (commanded by Allah) except for, they (must) worship Allah, purifiers (making pure, sincere and devoted) for Him (Allah) the Deen (religion, worship), (purely) devotees (HANIF- rejecter of all other false beliefs, only devoted to Allah) and they (were commanded to) they establish the prayers and they give Zakat (compulsory charity for poor) and that is the Deen (religion, way of life ordered by Allah)) upright (straight, strong and correct).

Aya 98:6

إِنَّ الَّذِينَ كَفَرُوا مِنْ أَهْلِ الْكِتَابِ وَالْمُشْرِكِينَ فِي نَارِ جَهَنَّمَ خَالِدِينَ فِيهَا أُولَٰئِكَ هُمْ شَرُّ الْبَرِيَّةِ

Surely, those who rejected (disbelieved Quran and the prophet Muhammad, peace be upon him) from the people of the book (Jews and Christians) and Polytheists (infidels of Makkah) will be in the fire of Hell, stayers (living) forever in it (in hellfire), those (people), they are the worst of living beings (creatures, animals walking on the dry non-sea earth).

Aya 98:7

إِنَّ الَّذِينَ آمَنُوا وَعَمِلُوا الصَّالِحَاتِ أُولَٰئِكَ هُمْ خَيْرُ الْبَرِيَّةِ

Surely, those who believed (in Allah's religion) and did good deeds, those people, are the best of living beings (creatures, animals walking on the dry, non-sea earth).

Aya 98:8

جَزَاؤُهُمْ عِندَ رَبِّهِمْ جَنَّاتُ عَدْنٍ تَجْرِي مِن تَحْتِهَا الْأَنْهَارُ خَالِدِينَ فِيهَا أَبَدًا رَّضِيَ اللَّهُ عَنْهُمْ وَرَضُوا عَنْهُ ذَٰلِكَ لِمَنْ خَشِيَ رَبَّهُ

Reward of theirs (true believers), with Lord of theirs, are gardens (paradise) of living forever (eternity), flowing underneath which are rivers, stayer (living) in it (paradise) forever, got pleased Allah from them (true believers) and they (true believers) got pleased from Him (Allah), that (paradise and pleasure of Allah) is for the one who feared Lord of his (Allah)

سُورَةُ الزَّلْزَلَةِ

Surat Al Zilzal

The Glorious Quran 99

بِسْمِ اللَّهِ الرَّحْمَٰنِ الرَّحِيمِ

(I begin) with the name of Allah, the Most Beneficent (Most Kind), the Most Merciful.

Aya 99:1
إِذَا زُلْزِلَتِ الْأَرْضُ زِلْزَالَهَا

(On the day of resurrection) When shaken, is the earth, shaking of it (earthquake).

Aya 99:2
وَأَخْرَجَتِ الْأَرْضُ أَثْقَالَهَا

And brought out (threw out) the earth, burdens of it (people buried in the earth are resurrected).

Aya 99:3
وَقَالَ الْإِنْسَانُ مَا لَهَا

And said the human, what is for it (what is the matter with the earth)?

Aya 99:4
يَوْمَئِذٍ تُحَدِّثُ أَخْبَارَهَا

That day (of resurrection), (earth) will talk about news (information) of it (about all that happened on earth, good or evil).

Aya 99:5
بِأَنَّ رَبَّكَ أَوْحَىٰ لَهَا

Because, (due to) that Lord of yours (Allah) revealed (inspired, commanded) for it (commanded the earth to disclose).

Aya 99:6
يَوْمَئِذٍ يَصْدُرُ النَّاسُ أَشْتَاتًا لِّيُرَوْا أَعْمَالَهُمْ

That day (of resurrection) will come forward (proceed) the people scattered (in groups) for to be shown to them deeds of theirs.

Aya 99:7
فَمَن يَعْمَلْ مِثْقَالَ ذَرَّةٍ خَيْرًا يَرَهُ

So, the one who does, weight of a small particle good (deed), he will see it.

Aya 99:8
وَمَن يَعْمَلْ مِثْقَالَ ذَرَّةٍ شَرًّا يَرَهُ

And the one who does, the weight of a small particle bad (deed), he will see it.

سُورَةُ الْعَادِيَاتِ

Surat Al A'adiyaat

The Glorious Quran 100

بِسْمِ اللَّهِ الرَّحْمَٰنِ الرَّحِيمِ

(I begin) with the name of Allah, the Most Beneficent (Most Kind), the Most Merciful.

Aya 100:1
وَالْعَادِيَاتِ ضَبْحًا

(I swear) by the gallopers (galloping, running fast horses), panting (making snorting noises).

Aya 100:2
فَالْمُورِيَاتِ قَدْحًا

So, (those galloping snorting horses are) strikers, sparks (by hitting stones on the ground with their hooves).

Aya 100:3
فَالْمُغِيرَاتِ صُبْحًا

So, (those galloping snorting horses are) raiders in the morning (at dawn).

Aya 100:4
فَأَثَرْنَ بِهِ نَقْعًا

So, (those galloping snorting horses are) trailing with it (with the running or the raid), dust (leaving dust along the way)

Aya 100:5

فَوَسَطْنَ بِهِ جَمْعًا

So, they get in the middle with it (with those dust blowing horses), (in) gathering (in the middle of the gathering of the opposing army).

Aya 100:6

إِنَّ الْإِنسَانَ لِرَبِّهِ لَكَنُودٌ

(Answer to all swearing) Surely, the human is, for Lord of his (Allah), definitely, ungrateful.

Aya 100:7

وَإِنَّهُ عَلَىٰ ذَٰلِكَ لَشَهِيدٌ

And surely, he (human) is on that (ungratefulness), definitely, a witness.

Aya 100:8

وَإِنَّهُ لِحُبِّ الْخَيْرِ لَشَدِيدٌ

And surely, he (human), for the love of the good (any good thing like money and authority), definitely, is intense.

Aya 100:9

أَفَلَا يَعْلَمُ إِذَا بُعْثِرَ مَا فِي الْقُبُورِ

Does not he (human) know, when overturned (spilled out, resurrected), is what is in the graves?

Aya 100:10

وَحُصِّلَ مَا فِي الصُّدُورِ

And obtained (exposed) is, what is in the chests (secrets of hearts are made known).

Aya 100:11

إِنَّ رَبَّهُم بِهِمْ يَوْمَئِذٍ لَّخَبِيرٌ

Surely, Lord of theirs (Allah), on them, that day, is definitely (all) Aware.

سُورَةُ القَارِعَةِ

Surat Al Qare'ah

The Glorious Quran 101

بِسْمِ اللَّهِ الرَّحْمَٰنِ الرَّحِيمِ

(I begin) with the name of Allah, the Most Beneficent (Most Kind), the Most Merciful.

Aya 101:1
الْقَارِعَةُ

The Al-Qari'ah (the striking calamity, the clatterer, the Day of Resurrection).

Aya 101:2
مَا الْقَارِعَةُ

What is the striking (calamity)?

Aya 101:3
وَمَا أَدْرَاكَ مَا الْقَارِعَةُ

And what made you know (understand), what is the striking (calamity)?

Aya 101:4
يَوْمَ يَكُونُ النَّاسُ كَالْفَرَاشِ الْمَبْثُوثِ

(The striking calamity or the day of judgment) That day will become the people like moths, the scattered (dispersed moths).

Aya 101:5
وَتَكُونُ الْجِبَالُ كَالْعِهْنِ الْمَنفُوشِ

And will become mountains like (colored) wool, carded (fluffed up, loosened).

Aya 101:6
فَأَمَّا مَن ثَقُلَتْ مَوَازِينُهُ

So, the one became heavy scales of his (the balance of good deeds is heavier).

Aya 101:7
فَهُوَ فِي عِيشَةٍ رَّاضِيَةٍ

So, he is in (a) living, pleasant (in a life of choice and pleasures in paradise).

Aya 101:8
وَأَمَّا مَنْ خَفَّتْ مَوَازِينُهُ

And the one became light scales (of good deeds) of his (the balance of good deeds is lighter).

Aya 101:9
فَأُمُّهُ هَاوِيَةٌ

So, mother of his (place of living or refuge of his) is Haawiya

Aya 101:10
وَمَا أَدْرَاكَ مَا هِيَهْ

And what made you know (understand) what it is (Haawiya)?

Aya 101:11
نَارٌ حَامِيَةٌ

(Haawiya is) Fire hot (blazing)

سُورَةُ التَّكَاثُرِ

Surat At Takathur

The Glorious Quran 102

بِسْمِ اللَّهِ الرَّحْمَٰنِ الرَّحِيمِ

(I begin) with the name of Allah, the Most Beneficent (Most Kind), the Most Merciful.

Aya 102:1
أَلْهَاكُمُ التَّكَاثُرُ

Distracted (diverted) you, the abundance (more wealth or struggle to collect more wealth, took you away from the remembrance of Allah).

Aya 102:2
حَتَّىٰ زُرْتُمُ الْمَقَابِرَ

Till you visited the graves (till death came to you).

Aya 102:3
كَلَّا سَوْفَ تَعْلَمُونَ

Nay (no, no, but), Soon will you know (come to know the reality).

Aya 102:4
ثُمَّ كَلَّا سَوْفَ تَعْلَمُونَ

Again, Nay (no, no, but), soon, will you know (come to know the reality).

Aya 102:5
كَلَّا لَوْ تَعْلَمُونَ عِلْمَ الْيَقِينِ

Nay (no, no, but) if you know, knowledge of the certainty.

Aya 102:6
لَتَرَوُنَّ الْجَحِيمَ

Definitely, you will see the hellfire.

Aya 102:7
ثُمَّ لَتَرَوُنَّهَا عَيْنَ الْيَقِينِ

Again, definitely, you will see it (the hellfire), (with the) eye of the certainty.

Aya 102:8
ثُمَّ لَتُسْأَلُنَّ يَوْمَئِذٍ عَنِ النَّعِيمِ

Then, definitely, you will be asked, that day (of judgment) from (about) the bounties (about all those good things that you were given by Allah in this world).

سُورَةُ العَصْرِ

Surat Al A'sr

The Glorious Quran 103

بِسْمِ اللَّهِ الرَّحْمَٰنِ الرَّحِيمِ

(I begin) with the name of Allah, the Most Beneficent (Most Kind), the Most Merciful.

Aya 103:1

وَالْعَصْرِ

(Swear) By the Asr (the time, the generation, the time of late afternoon prayer).

Aya 103:2

إِنَّ الْإِنسَانَ لَفِي خُسْرٍ

Surely, the humans (mankind) are definitely in (a) loss.

Aya 103:3

إِلَّا الَّذِينَ آمَنُوا وَعَمِلُوا الصَّالِحَاتِ وَتَوَاصَوْا بِالْحَقِّ وَتَوَاصَوْا بِالصَّبْرِ

Except those who believed (in Allah) and did the good deeds and advised (counseled others) with the truth and advised (counseled others) with the patience.

سُورَةُ الهُمَزَةِ

Surat Al Humazah

The Glorious Quran 104

بِسْمِ اللَّهِ الرَّحْمَٰنِ الرَّحِيمِ

(I begin) with the name of Allah, the Most Beneficent (Most Kind), the Most Merciful.

Aya 104:1
وَيْلٌ لِّكُلِّ هُمَزَةٍ لُّمَزَةٍ

Woe (destruction) for every (all) slanderer (accuser, faultfinder) and defamer (backbiter).

Aya 104:2
الَّذِي جَمَعَ مَالًا وَعَدَّدَهُ

The one (who) gathered wealth and counted it (the wealth).

Aya 104:3
يَحْسَبُ أَنَّ مَالَهُ أَخْلَدَهُ

(The money-hoarding slanderer person) Thinks that wealth of his will make him immortal (lasting forever).

Aya 104:4
كَلَّا ۖ لَيُنبَذَنَّ فِي الْحُطَمَةِ

Nay (no, no but) definitely, (the money hoarding slanderer person) will be thrown into the Hutamah (the crushing fire).

Aya 104:5
وَمَا أَدْرَاكَ مَا الْحُطَمَةُ

And what made you know, what is the Hutamah (the crushing Fire)?

Aya 104:6

نَارُ اللَّهِ الْمُوقَدَةُ

(Hutamah is) Fire of Allah kindled (fueled to burn).

Aya 104:7

الَّتِي تَطَّلِعُ عَلَى الْأَفْئِدَةِ

The one (fire that) peeps (gets, reaches) over the hearts.

Aya 104:8

إِنَّهَا عَلَيْهِم مُّؤْصَدَةٌ

Surely, this (fire) on them will be closed (imposed).

Aya 104:9

فِي عَمَدٍ مُّمَدَّدَةٍ

(Fire imposed on them) In pillars (columns) stretched (in extended, long columns).

سُورَةُ الفِيلِ

Surat Al Feel

The Glorious Quran 105

بِسْمِ اللَّهِ الرَّحْمَٰنِ الرَّحِيمِ

(I begin) with the name of Allah, the Most Beneficent (Most Kind), the Most Merciful.

Aya 105:1

أَلَمْ تَرَ كَيْفَ فَعَلَ رَبُّكَ بِأَصْحَابِ الْفِيلِ

Have not, you seen, how did (dealt with), Lord of yours (Allah) with the companions of the elephant?

Aya 105:2

أَلَمْ يَجْعَلْ كَيْدَهُمْ فِي تَضْلِيلٍ

Did not He (Allah) make the plot of theirs in misguidance (in error, wasted, failed)?

Aya 105:3

وَأَرْسَلَ عَلَيْهِمْ طَيْرًا أَبَابِيلَ

And He (Allah) sent on them birds, in flocks (swarms).

Aya 105:4

تَرْمِيهِم بِحِجَارَةٍ مِّن سِجِّيلٍ

Striking them (companions of the elephant) with stones from baked clay.

Aya 105:5

فَجَعَلَهُمْ كَعَصْفٍ مَّأْكُولٍ

So, He (Allah made) them like straw (hay, chaff), eaten up.

سُورَةُ قُرَيْشٍ

Surat Al Quraysh

The Glorious Quran 106

بِسْمِ اللَّهِ الرَّحْمَٰنِ الرَّحِيمِ

(I begin) with the name of Allah, the Most Beneficent (Most Kind), the Most Merciful.

Aya 106:1
لِإِيلَافِ قُرَيْشٍ

For the liking (familiarity, consolation) of Quraish (the tribe of Quraish in Makkah).

Aya 106:2
إِيلَافِهِمْ رِحْلَةَ الشِّتَاءِ وَالصَّيْفِ

Liking (familiarity) of theirs (Quraish for) the travel (trade visits) of the winter and the summer.

Aya 106:3
فَلْيَعْبُدُوا رَبَّ هَٰذَا الْبَيْتِ

So, they should worship the Lord of this House (Kaaba, Allah is Lord of Kaaba, the house of Allah).

Aya 106:4
الَّذِي أَطْعَمَهُم مِّن جُوعٍ وَآمَنَهُم مِّنْ خَوْفٍ

The One (Allah) who fed them (Quraish) from hunger and secured them (Quraish) from fear.

سُورَةُ المَاعُونِ

Surat Al Maau'n

The Glorious Quran 107

بِسْمِ اللَّهِ الرَّحْمَٰنِ الرَّحِيمِ

(I begin) with the name of Allah, the Most Beneficent (Most Kind), the Most Merciful

Aya 107:1
أَرَأَيْتَ الَّذِي يُكَذِّبُ بِالدِّينِ

Have you seen the one who belies (rejects as a lie, denies) the Deen (religion of Islam or the day of judgment)?

Aya 107:2
فَذَٰلِكَ الَّذِي يَدُعُّ الْيَتِيمَ

So that is the one who pushes away (repulses, mistreats) the orphan (is harsh with, does not take care of an orphan).

Aya 107:3
وَلَا يَحُضُّ عَلَىٰ طَعَامِ الْمِسْكِينِ

And does not he urge (encourages others) on food (for) the poor.

Aya 107:4
فَوَيْلٌ لِّلْمُصَلِّينَ

So, woe (destruction) is for the praying (people).

Aya 107:5
الَّذِينَ هُمْ عَن صَلَاتِهِمْ سَاهُونَ

Those (praying people) who are, from the prayer of theirs, neglectful (unaware).

Aya 107:6
الَّذِينَ هُمْ يُرَاءُونَ

Those who show off (do good deeds to show off and not exclusively for the sake of Allah).

Aya 107:7
وَيَمْنَعُونَ الْمَاعُونَ

And they refuse (deny giving others) the small objects of need.

سُورَةُ الكَوثَرِ

Surat Al Kauthar

The Glorious Quran 108

بِسْمِ اللَّهِ الرَّحْمَٰنِ الرَّحِيمِ

(I begin) with the name of Allah, the Most Beneficent (Most Kind), the Most Merciful.

Aya 108:1
إِنَّا أَعْطَيْنَاكَ الْكَوْثَرَ

Surely, We (Allah) gave you (O prophet Muhammad, peace be upon him) the Al-Kauthar (a spring/river in paradise).

Aya 108:2
فَصَلِّ لِرَبِّكَ وَانْحَرْ

So, pray (only) for the Lord of yours (Allah) and do (practice) sacrifice (of animals for the sake of Allah, in Haj and Eid ul Adha).

Aya 108:3
إِنَّ شَانِئَكَ هُوَ الْأَبْتَرُ

Surely, the enemy of yours, (O prophet Muhammad, peace be upon him), is the one cut off (curtailed, with no posterity, with no one to remember him afterward).

سُورَةُ الْكَافِرُونَ

Surat Al Kafiroon

The Glorious Quran 109

بِسْمِ اللَّهِ الرَّحْمَٰنِ الرَّحِيمِ

(I begin) with the name of Allah, the Most Beneficent (Most Kind), the Most Merciful.

Aya 109:1

قُلْ يَا أَيُّهَا الْكَافِرُونَ

Say (O Prophet Muhammad, peace be upon him) O you, the disbelievers (Rejecters of Islam).

Aya 109:2

لَا أَعْبُدُ مَا تَعْبُدُونَ

Not I worship what you (disbelievers) are worshiping.

Aya 109:3

وَلَا أَنتُمْ عَابِدُونَ مَا أَعْبُدُ

And not are you (disbelievers), worshipers of what I (Prophet Muhammad, peace be upon him) worship.

Aya 109:4

وَلَا أَنَا عَابِدٌ مَّا عَبَدتُّمْ

And not am I (Prophet Muhammad, peace be upon him) worshiper of what you (disbelievers) worshiped.

Aya 109:5

وَلَا أَنتُمْ عَابِدُونَ مَا أَعْبُدُ

And not are you (disbelievers), worshipers of what I (Prophet Muhammad, peace be upon him) worship.

Aya 109:6

لَكُمْ دِينُكُمْ وَلِيَ دِينِ

For you (disbelievers) is the religion of yours, and for me (Prophet Muhammad, peace be upon him) is the religion of mine.

سُورَةُ النَّصْرِ

Surat Al Nasr

The Glorious Quran 110

بِسْمِ اللَّهِ الرَّحْمَٰنِ الرَّحِيمِ

(I begin) with the name of Allah, the Most Beneficent (Most Kind), the Most Merciful.

Aya 110:1
إِذَا جَاءَ نَصْرُ اللَّهِ وَالْفَتْحُ

When came the help of Allah and the victory (conquest of Makkah).

Aya 110:2
وَرَأَيْتَ النَّاسَ يَدْخُلُونَ فِي دِينِ اللَّهِ أَفْوَاجًا

And you saw the people entering the Deen (religion, way of life) of Allah (Islam) in groups (droves, crowds).

Aya 110:3
فَسَبِّحْ بِحَمْدِ رَبِّكَ وَاسْتَغْفِرْهُ إِنَّهُ كَانَ تَوَّابًا

So proclaim purity (glorify) with praise of Lord of yours (Allah), and pray (ask for) forgiveness of His (Allah); surely, He (Allah) was (is) very (highly) accepter of the repentance (and forgives).

سُورَةُ المَسَدِ

Surat Al Masad

The Glorious Quran 111

بِسْمِ اللَّهِ الرَّحْمَٰنِ الرَّحِيمِ

(I begin) with the name of Allah, the Most Beneficent (Most Kind), the Most Merciful.

Aya 111:1

تَبَّتْ يَدَا أَبِي لَهَبٍ وَتَبَّ

Be destroyed (perished) both hands of Abu Lahab (disbeliever uncle of Prophet Muhammad, peace be upon him, who was cursing and slandering) and got destroyed (perished).

Aya 111:2

مَا أَغْنَىٰ عَنْهُ مَالُهُ وَمَا كَسَبَ

Did not benefit (did not save, did not remove) from him, wealth of his (Abu Lahab) and not (benefited him) what he earned (did).

Aya 111:3

سَيَصْلَىٰ نَارًا ذَاتَ لَهَبٍ

Soon, he (Abu Lahab) will reach fire with (blazing) flames.

Aya 111:4

وَامْرَأَتُهُ حَمَّالَةَ الْحَطَبِ

And woman (wife) of his, carrier of the firewood

Aya 111:5

فِي جِيدِهَا حَبْلٌ مِّن مَّسَدٍ

In the neck of her (wife of Abu Lahab will be) rope (made) from palm fiber.

سُورَةُ الإِخْلَاصِ

Surat Al Ikhlaas

The Glorious Quran 112

بِسْمِ اللَّهِ الرَّحْمَٰنِ الرَّحِيمِ

(I begin) with the name of Allah, the Most Beneficent (Most Kind), the Most Merciful.

Aya 112:1
قُلْ هُوَ اللَّهُ أَحَدٌ

Say (O Prophet Muhammad, peace be upon him) He is the Allah, the One (with no partners of any kind, ever).

Aya 112:2
اللَّهُ الصَّمَدُ

Allah -The Self-Sufficient (all creatures need Allah, but Allah does not need anyone).

Aya 112:3
لَمْ يَلِدْ وَلَمْ يُولَدْ

He (Allah) does not give birth (to anyone, has no children), and not was He (Allah) given birth to.
(He begets not, nor is He begotten).

Aya 112:4
وَلَمْ يَكُنْ لَهُ كُفُوًا أَحَدٌ

And not is there, for Him (Allah) equal (comparable) anyone.

سُورَةُ الفَلَقِ

Surat Al Falaq

The Glorious Quran 113

بِسْمِ اللَّهِ الرَّحْمَٰنِ الرَّحِيمِ

(I begin) with the name of Allah, the Most Beneficent (Most Kind), the Most Merciful.

Aya 113:1
قُلْ أَعُوذُ بِرَبِّ الْفَلَقِ

Say (O Prophet Muhammad, Peace be upon him) I seek refuge with the Lord (Allah) of the daybreak (dawn).

Aya 113:2
مِن شَرِّ مَا خَلَقَ

From the evil (hurt, harm, bad effects) of what He (Allah) created.

Aya 113:3
وَمِن شَرِّ غَاسِقٍ إِذَا وَقَبَ

And (I seek refuge) from the evil (hurt, harm, bad effects) of the darkness, when it (the darkness) spread (becomes intense).

Aya 113:4
وَمِن شَرِّ النَّفَّاثَاتِ فِي الْعُقَدِ

And (I seek refuge) from the evil (hurt, harm, bad effects) of blowing women in the knots (doing witchcraft and magic and blowing after their utterings into knots of clothes, threads, or hairs).

Aya 113:5

وَمِن شَرِّ حَاسِدٍ إِذَا حَسَدَ

And (I seek refuge) from the evil (hurt, harm, and bad effects) of the jealous (one, the envious person) when he practiced jealousy (envied).

سُورَةُ النَّاسِ

Surat Al Naas

The Glorious Quran 114

بِسْمِ اللَّهِ الرَّحْمَٰنِ الرَّحِيمِ

(I begin) with the name of Allah, the Most Beneficent (Most Kind), the Most Merciful.

Aya 114:1
قُلْ أَعُوذُ بِرَبِّ النَّاسِ

Say (O Prophet Muhammad, peace be upon him) I seek refuge with the Lord of the people (Allah).

Aya 114:2
مَلِكِ النَّاسِ

The King (ultimate authority) of the people.

Aya 114:3
إِلَٰهِ النَّاسِ

The Elah (GOD, worthy of the worship) of the people.

Aya 114:4
مِن شَرِّ الْوَسْوَاسِ الْخَنَّاسِ

(I Seek refuge) From the evil (hurt, harm, bad effects) of the whisperings (doubtful, disturbing, and intruding thoughts) of the withdrawer (Shaitaan or devil that runs away or withdraws after whispering bad thoughts).

Aya 114:5
اَلَّذِي يُوَسْوِسُ فِي صُدُورِ النَّاسِ

The one (Shaitaan, the devil) who whispers (introduces bad thoughts) into the chests (hearts) of the people.

Aya 114:6
مِنَ الْجِنَّةِ وَالنَّاسِ

(Shaitaans, or devils) From Jinns (ghosts, non-visible creations of Allah with intelligence) and (devils from) the people (humans).